A Gabriela Mistral Reader

Translated by Maria Giachetti

Edited by Marjorie Agosin

WHITE PINE PRESS

Publication of this book was made possible, in part,
by grants from the National Endowment for the Arts,
the New York State Council on the Arts,
and Wellesley College.

Book design: Watershed Design

ISBN 1-877727-18-0

First printing, 1993

10   9   8   7   6   5   4   3   2

Published by White Pine Press
10 Village Square
Fredonia, New York 14063

A Gabriela Mistral Reader

Acknowledgements

I would like to thank Dennis Maloney for presenting me with the opportunity to translate Mistral. During the course of this project, his vision and confidence have helped energize my efforts. In addition, I would like to thank Marjorie Agosin, who served as an editor, reader, and friend. Because of the insight of Dennis and Marjorie, Gabriela Mistral's work is once again in print in English.

I would also like to extend my thanks to Dr. Elizabeth Nelson and Lewis Livesay of Saint Peter's College, and to Celeste Kostopulus-Cooperman, and Susana Gazek for serving as readers of the manuscript.

—Maria Giachetti

I would like to thank all of those in Chile and throughout the world who have kept the poetry, vision, and spirit of Gabriela Mistral alive, including Roque Esteban Scarpa, Jaime Quezada, Santiago Dairdy, Eliana Ortega, Elizabeth Horan, and Doris Dana.

Special thanks to Celeste Kostopulus-Cooperman for her careful reading of the manuscript and her valuable suggestions. Also to the translator, Maria Giachetti, for her dedication to rendering in English the beauty and power of Mistral's Spanish. A word of *gracias* to Dennis Maloney, editor of White Pine Press, for his encouragement of this project since the very beginning.

—Marjorie Agosin
Wellesley College

Contents

Poetry

Section I - Desolation

Section II - Tenderness

Section V - Poem of Chile

Prose

A Gabriela Mistral Reader

Gabriela Mistral, the Restless Soul

Gabriela Mistral's name evokes a constellation of contradictory images: a rural schoolteacher and recipient of the Nobel Prize in Literature, a poet who sang to children but never had any of her own, a provincialist and a universal traveler. All these references to her mythic image contain some truth and form part of the legacy of Gabriela Mistral, the first Latin American Nobel laureate, and the only Latin American woman to date to receive this prize. Little of her prodigious body of work has been translated into other languages. Most lies hidden, almost unexplored by the readers who are familiar only with her first book, *Desolación* (1922), which was published originally in the United States, and with poems disseminated in magazines and anthologies.

One cannot talk about Gabriela Mistral without discussing the landscape of her childhood. She was raised in Montegrande, a small village in northern Chile's Elqui Valley, surrounded by the pre-Andean winds of the cordillera, by the implacable sun, and by figs. The countryside of Montegrande, of the Elqui Valley, was Biblical and magical. "I left behind a labyrinth of hills, and something of this knot which cannot be unravelled remains in what I create, whether verse or prose," she later confessed. This "labyrinth of hills" was the space where she was initiated into poetry and where her language was tapestried with exalted Biblical references learned from her grandmother's lips. It was also where she completely dedicated herself to the vocation and avocation that would form the basis of her life: teacher and traveler.

Mistral's biography might seem to be a kind of deep fiction, lending itself to the mystification and invention of its very essence. Born Lucila Godoy de Alcayaga into the heart of a humble family, she began her teaching career in 1905 at the age of fifteen, without benefit of a teaching certificate, in the village of La Compañiá, located not far from her childhood home. After obtaining her teaching certificate, she taught in secondary schools in various places in Chile. In 1914, under the pseudonyn Gabriela Mistral, a name derived from the Archangel Gabriel and from the cold, dry wind that blows across the south of France, she entered a trio of sonnets, "Los Sonetos de la Muerte," in a national poetry contest. Her "Sonnets of Death" won the Chilean national prize for poetry. By 1917 her published poems and stories had made her an established national literary figure, and she was noticed by the Chilean Ministry of Education, which waived degree requirements and appointed her principal in public schools, first in Punta Arenas, the planet's southern-most city, and later in Temuco. While serving in Temuco she was frequently visited by the sixteen-year-old poet who would later be renowned as Pablo Neruda and sparked his interest in reading the Russian masters.

In 1922, having achieved a measure of fame in France, Spain, and Latin America, she traveled to Mexico at the request of the Mexican Minister of Education, Jose Vasconcelos, to assist in organizing the country's educational reforms. The Mexican people received her enthusiastically. While in Mexico she compiled an interesting prose collection, *Lecturas para mujeres*, written specifically to help educate female readers, and her first book of poetry, *Desolación (Desolation)*, was published in New York City, transcending the Latin American frontier.

In 1924 Mistral left Mexico and traveled extensively in the United States, France, Spain, Italy, and back to the land of her birth. Everywhere she went, the brown-skirted teacher with green eyes and an Indian face made an impact, charming and intriguing whomever she encountered. Her presence, according to so many, was both aesthetic and primitive. She was a woman of her country and of the world, a solitary and yet public woman. Her love of country and the Americas was immortalized in Poema de Chile, published posthumously in 1967.

She published three additional books during her lifetime: *Ternura (Tenderness)*, Madrid, 1924; *Tala (Felling)*, Buenos Aires, 1938; and *Lagar (Wine Press)*, Santiago, Chile, 1954, and taught briefly as a visiting professor at Barnard, Mills, Middlebury, Vassar, and the University of Puerto Rico. For twenty years, beginning in 1933, she was Chilean consul, serving in Madrid, Lisbon, Naples, Los Angeles, and various other cities. She chose to spend the last few years of her life in the United States. She died in New York in 1957 and was buried in her beloved Montegrande. The inscription on her tomb reads, "What the soul does for the body so does the poet for her people."

This epitaph voices Mistral's essence and her intrinsic connection with all marginalized people. In an interview given after receiving the Nobel, Prize she affirmed that perhaps she was given this prize "...because I was the candidate of the women and children." Mistral's reality and personal mythology are clearly stated in this sentence. She was perpetually aware of speaking for the voiceless and the silenced. The source of this voice was a nonauthoritarian power arising from Mistral's identification with Christ's dolorous suffering and her recognition of its purifying nature. Yet at the same time, she spoke from a political platform, disguised as the brown-skirted teacher wearing men's shoes, the humble woman who somehow crossed the cordillera and arrived in distant Stockholm to be awarded the Nobel Prize. She managed this dual persona by instilling soul and resonance into a language as regional as it was universal. Certainly, this disguise and her perpetual humble gestures permitted Gabriela Mistral to invent a persona uniquely her own.

Mistral's poetic text consisted mostly of Chilean geography, the Elqui Valley, and the arid and fertile North. It was a text that claimed cosmic and universal territory. The poet, therefore, chose to make her voice psalmic and prophetic: "I dreamt about a fig tree of the Elqui that yielded an abundance of milk in my house. The countryside was dry, the stones, thirsty…"

The Elqui Valley, Chilean women and children, created Gabriela Mistral's voice; it sprang from her very depths, and was destined for the exterior world. Her provincialism became universalized, but she established herself and clearly defined her position as an "outsider" in the capital's intellectual circles. These groups often welcomed and helped her, although they regarded her appearance with a certain suspicion. In harmony with the image of a rustic woman, Gabriela Mistral created a singular language in Latin American speech, which, according to the noted Chilean poet Enrique Litin, was "without precedent, without a previous school, and without heirs." Gabriela Mistral's language, in poetry, in prose, or in newspaper articles, has no equal. It possesses the intensity of the mystic Judeo-Christian poetic tradition and invokes earthly things—nature, the Indian world, female culture—in all their harmony and dissidence and yet it exhibits a keen sense of modernity.

Gabriela Mistral remained a phenomenon who fascinated her biographers as much as her readers. She was given the stigma of the ugly, old, and masculine schoolteacher. She was also labelled a foreigner, which enabled her to obtain official power and recognition. Certainly, Mistral created her own public image in those places where she was regarded suspiciously. More than her biography, we should understand the personality that helped her to forge a poetic identity, what we call "the woman on the outside," the stranger capable of assuming the identity created in the poem.

Mistral knew how to manipulate her own image, concealing rebellion under the mask of the rural schoolteacher to create through her poetry a strong identity as a teacher, the traditional image of one who shares knowledge with others. But behind that image was the daring poet: the innovator was the teacher who refused to be authoritarian and the one who chose her own identity and voice, bonding herself with children, with women, with the humble, and with social action. She relinquished the traditional to invent a language distant from the flowery language of the epoch.

In her writing and in her being, Mistral rebelled against her role of submissive teacher. When she held important public posts, Mistral was always the stranger who appeared overwhelmed, but whom, upon speaking, removed her mask and produced an open, ample, and unrestricted text which she characterized as "Saudade," using the Portugese word meaning "nostalgia." Gabriela Mistral stated, "I have written as I speak—in solitude," but at the same time that she assumed the role of a solitary rural woman in her poetry and writing process, she declared, "I write on my knees in a little tablet with which I always travel, and the desk-table has never been of any use to me—not in Chile, Paris or Lisbon."

Gabriela Mistral was a kind of visionary sibyl, a wise woman whose wisdom implies an inner search, a sojourn on Earth, and also the possibility of self-empowerment through words. She achieved this by leaving the Elqui Valley and traveling through the immense Indian American countryside. But she did not only amplify the landscape of her birth; rather, she began to expand the landscape of Judeo-Christian tradition where words interlaced: images of corn, like those of the Bible, joined with the God of the Judeo-Christian tradition and with the beliefs of the Jewish mystics and Christians.

Gabriela Mistral was very Chilean and provincial, and yet she was universal. She represents one of the most original voices in Latin American poetry. Her work will always walk the edge between the ordinary place where she created her own myth as rural schoolteacher and the place where she allowed herself the luxury of being the delirious woman of free fantasy, especially in the group of poems titled "Mujeres locas" (Mad Women) from the book *Lagar*. Delirium became a posture, a mask demonstrating the limitations of thought. Mistral gives us texts where women posess an equalled, magical wisdom, an ancient knowledge, and it is a knowledge that is initiated in a unique, pleasant language, unattached to earthly things. At times in her poems, she interchanges the words of the crazy woman and the normal woman and in this way frees herself from all possible stereotypes; she becomes a prophetess who sings and travels. Her subject matter is spoken in the voice of a free woman with her own identity.

Gabriela Mistral wrote poems, prose, vignettes, stories to be read aloud, cradle songs, political texts, and literary criticism. Nevertheless, the most daring critics have never tried to discover what was behind the myth of the teacher who commented that her words were "unschooled" and "unrestrained." To date, her complete works are not edited. Her prose is hardly known outside of Chile, and few books are dedicated to her work. Her one-hundreth birthday was commemorated in 1989 by only a small celebration in Santiago, Chile. The male-dominated press has tended to regard her work as that of an eccentric feminist.

Despite the fact that Gabriela Mistral lived many years in the United States, the fact that *Desolación* was published in the states, and many of her unedited documents, letters, and personal papers belong to the Barnard College library, her work is practically unknown here. To date, there exists a collection of her poetry translated by Langston Hughes and a selection translated by Doris Dana. There is so much left to discover. The life of Gabriela Mistral, the footprints of her restless soul, her comings and goings, her absence from Chile for more than thirty years, have made her a mysterious and hermetic figure, known and unknown at the same time. There still remains much to decipher, to extract the myth of a myth, the mystery of the mother without children. One must begin to read Mistral, look for her, to get closer to her austere language, her American and cosmic nature, her landscape of words which exalts the elements of Earth with a modality and articulation unequalled in American language.

This anthology, translated by Maria Giachetti, represents, in my view, an important contribution to recognition of Mistral's genius. It is the first attempt to translate the broad spectrum of

Mistral's work. The selection comes together in varied form, gathered from Mistral's collected poems, cradle songs, and selections from other special works. A selection from the "Mujeres locas" section of *Lagar* is also included, as well as an important selection of her prose, which is difficult to find, even in Chile, since limited editions went out of print and have never been reprinted.

The purpose of this anthology is to make known her vast work by choosing those texts that exemplify the variety and originality of her intense literary production. A selection of her most representative prose is included; emphasis is given to her political writings and visions of important Latin American personalities such as her contemporary, Pablo Neruda, and some of her favorite writers.

The selection demonstrates Gabriela Mistral's extensive legacy from her beginnings in Northern Chile to her journeys across the American continent. Mistral, herself, is a vast landscape. But her fatherland is more than Chilean territory; rather, it implies a feeling, a way of communicating and inhabiting a world that is Indian, *mestizo* and genuinely American. She also imbues the concept of the fatherland with a feminine and the anti-hierarchial vision. The countryside is the center of Gabriela's identity; therefore, the Elqui Valley is her face and tongue.

Through Maria Giachetti's beautiful and skillfully realized translations, the reader will perceive the glimmering words of an Andean and Indian American woman, a defender of the poor, the perpetual stranger, the restless soul who begins with *Desolación* to speak and sing about the pain of an abandoned woman whose identity was forged by postponement, perpetual solitude and rejection.

More than gathering together Mistral's poetic texts and prose, this collection ultimately allows one to know her lyric universe, her zones of pain and shadow, her spaces of love and delirium, with all the transparency and joy that exists in poetry which mirrors life. She said, "Writing tends to cheer me. It always soothes my spirit and blesses me with an innocent, tender, child-like day."

—Marjorie Agosín
Wellesley College

Translator's Note

As a translator, I have discovered, that I change after each translation. It is a kind of almost haphazard development, something not the least bit scientific; instead alchemy comes to mind. I think that Gabriela Mistral would understand this rather strange feeling—the very root of it is a mystical reverence for language, a belief that words come to us packed with ordinary power, and this is a kind of magic. In writing which flows from the heart, the reader can be transformed. Gabriela Mistral's mission was transformation; I speak as one transformed.

Translation can be a more intimate and nitty gritty experience than reading. One must somehow get inside the poem and inhabit it. A verbal transfusion should happen. The hard walls of language and "otherness" shatter, or melt, or evanesce. The poem being translated becomes air, food, water, sun, everything. Both the original poem and the translation find homes in the translator's head. And if the translator is also a writer, the most fertile rain drenches her projects in embryonic stages.

Obviously, I want to thank the ever-present spirit of Gabriela Mistral, who has given me so much. I began reading Mistral when I was fourteen. I was learning Spanish, and she became one of my first teachers. Through the years, her work has followed me and embodied a subtle yet potent presence.

In translating this book, I felt a strong obligation to preserve and convey Mistral's sense of sacred, ordinary language, the inner rhythms of the Earth and its children. In Mistral's cosmos, plain words prevailed. She wanted to be understood by everyone since she most often spoke for the silent and the silenced.

Much of the world presented in this book seems to have vanished like the heart of the rain forest. Yet, Mistral grapples with the question of extinction in many forms, ranging from the genocide of Indians to the dismemberment of the planet.

Mistral's visions challenge historical shifts and surface changes. She was concerned with internal life, with mapping the mind's labyrinthine possibilities, the heart's geography—quests we all share.

—Maria Giachetti
Hazleton, Pennsylvania
1992

Poetry

Desolation

THE FUTURE

Winter will make white circles
over my afflicted heart.
Daylight will irritate;
I'll hurt myself with each song.

My forehead will grow weary of hair
parted straight and soft.
The scent of June violets
will be allowed to wither.

My mother will already have ten palms
of ashes over her temples.
No child, blond as corn,
will grow tall between my knees.

Prowling the tombs,
I won't see a sky or a wheat field.
By their removal, my crazed heart
will sleep.

And so the traces
of what I am searching for
dissipate into confusion,
but when I penetrate the Wide Light,
I won't have to discover it
ever again.

DROPS OF GALL

Don't sing: your tongue
always remains bound to a song:
the one that should be surrendered.

Don't kiss: by a strange curse
the kiss that does not reach
the heart, remains.

Pray, for prayer is sweet
but know that your greedy tongue
stumbles over the only "Our Father"
that might save you.

Don't call death kind,
for within its immense white flesh
a live fragment will remain and feel
the stone that smothers you
and the voracious worm that unbraids your hair.

THE PRISON SENTENCE

Oh fountain of pale turquoise!
Oh rose tree in fiery flower!
How can I break off your blazing flame
and sink my lips into your freshness!

Deep fountain of loving,
fiery rose tree of kisses,
death commands us to march
to its bony chamber.

The clear and implacable voice calls
from the deep night,
and during the day
from its box of miseries.

Oh, fountain, the fresh lips close—
a drink would have given wings to that one
who has fallen to Earth.

THE VIGILANT WOMAN

Since I am a queen and I was once a beggar,
I now live with the pure fear of your leaving me,
and pale, I ask you at all hours,
"Are you still with me? Oh, please don't abandon me!"

I would like to move ahead smiling
and trusting now that you've come,
but even in sleep I'm afraid
and ask between dreams, "Haven't you left?"

THE BONES OF THE DEAD

The bones of the dead are tender ice
that knows how to crumble
and become dust on the lips
of the ones who loved them.
And these live lips can no longer kiss.

The bones of the dead
swiftly
spread their whiteness
over life's intense flame.
They kill all passion!

The bones of the dead
can do more than living flesh.
Even disjointed, they make mighty chains,
keeping us submissive and captive.

BALLAD

He passed by with another woman;
I saw him pass by.
The wind was forever sweet
and the road, peaceful.
And these wretched eyes
beheld him passing by!

He continues loving another woman
into flowery lands.
The hawthorn has bloomed;
a song slips away.
And he continues loving another woman
into flowery lands.

He kissed the other woman
on seashores;
the orange blossom moon
trembled upon the waves.
And my blood did not annoint
the expansive sea!

He will walk with another woman
into eternity.
Sweet skies will prevail.
(God desires silence.)
He will journey with another woman
through eternity!

THE OBSESSION

He touches me in the nocturnal dew;
he bleeds in sunsets.
He searches for me with moonbeams
through caverns.

Like Christ with Thomas,
he sinks my pale hand
into his wet wound
so that I will not forget.

I have told him
that I want to die,
but he does not wish it
to touch me in the wind,
to cover me with snow.

Moving through my dreams
like a face's flower,
he calls me through the green
handkerchief of trees.

And if I altered heaven?
I went to the sea and mountain,
and he walked to my edge,
and was my guest at inns.

You were an enshrouded, neglected woman.
You did not close his eyelids
or adjust his arms in the casket.

GOD WILLS IT

I

The Earth will become a wicked stepmother
if your soul sells my soul.
Waters carry a chill of tribulation.
The world has become more splendid
since you made me your ally in love,
when beside a hawthorn
we remained without words:
and love, like the thorny tree,
pierced us with fragrance!

But the Earth will make your body
bloom with snakes
if you sell my soul.
I will crush these desolate knees
that hold no child.
The radiant Christ within my heart
will be extinguished;
the hand of the homeless wanderer
will be broken
and the anguished woman will be
driven from the door of my house.

II

The kiss you give to another
will reach my ears
because deep caverns return
your words to me.
The dust of roadways
guards the scent of your footsteps.
Like a deer, I will follow them

through the mountains.

Above my house,
the clouds will paint the image
of the one you adore.
Thief! You will have to hide
to kiss her in the bowels of the Earth,
and when you lift her face,
you will see my face, wet with tears.

III

God does not desire sun in your life
if you do not walk with me.
God does not want you to enjoy refreshment
if I do not tremble in your waters.
He only wants you to sleep
next to my gathered braids.

IV

If you go away,
you will trample my soul,
even in the moss upon the road.
Thirst and hunger
will sink their teeth into you
on every mountain or plain,
and in every country
bloody afternoons will display my wounds.

And my name will fall in drops
from your tongue although you speak
the name of another woman,
and in your throat, I will nail myself,
a briny vestige.

And when you hate or sing or worry,
you will only clamor for me!

V

If you go away from me
and perish in a distant land,
your cupped hand
will receive my tears
for ten years under the earth.
You will feel how my miserable flesh
trembles for you
until my bones shatter and spread
their dust over your face.

THE ARTIST'S DECALOGUE

    I. You will cherish Beauty, God's shadow over the universe.

    II. There is no art without God. Although you say that you do not love the Creator, you will affirm Him by creating His likeness.

    III. You will not create beauty as bait for the senses, but rather, you will create the soul's natural nourishment.

    IV. Beauty will not be your excuse for luxury or vanity; it is a divine exercise.

    V. You will not search for Beauty at carnivals, and you will not bring your work to them because Beauty is virginal, and what you find at carnivals does not belong in Beauty's realm.

    VI. Beauty will rise from your heart into your song, and you will be the first soul purified.

    VII. Your Beauty will also be called compassion and you will console the human heart.

    VIII. You will give birth to your work in the same way that a child is born: by subtracting the blood of your heart.

    IX. Your Beauty will not be a sleep-rendering opiate, but rather, a generous wine that inflames your actions. If you cease being a genuine man or woman, you will no longer be an artist.

    X. You will walk away from each creation with a sense of modesty because it was inferior to your dream, and inferior to God's marvelous dream: Nature.

THE USELESS VIGIL

I forgot that your light foot
was transformed into ashes,
and, as during good times,
I ventured to find you
along the path.

I passed through valley,
plain and river;
songs filled me with melancholy.
Afternoon faded,
tumbled its luminous vase.
And you didn't appear!

The sun crumbled its poppy,
charred and lifeless.
A foggy fringe trembled
over the fields.
I was alone!

From a tree,
a whitened branch like an arm,
rustled in the autumn wind.
I was terrified and cried out to you,
"My love, hurry to my side!"

"I hold fear
and I hold onto love.
My love, speed your journey!"
Night thickened around me;
my madness grew.

I forgot—they made you deaf
to my lament;

your deadly dawn,

your heavy hand,
too late, its quest for my hand,
and your wide eyes,
a sovereign inquisition!

Night extended
its bituminous-black pool;
The owl of mystic fortune
fretted the path
with the macabre silk
of its wings.
I will not call out to you again;
your journey has ended.
My naked foot continues its trek;
your foot remains eternally quiet.

In vain I hold this vigil
along deserted roads.
Your ghost will not come together
in my open arms!

TO SEE HIM AGAIN

Never, never again?
Not on nights filled with quivering stars,
or during dawn's maiden brightness
or afternoons of sacrifice?

Or at the edge of a pale path
that encircles the farmlands,
or upon the rim of a trembling fountain,
whitened by a shimmering moon?

Or beneath the forest's
luxuriant, raveled tresses
where, calling his name,
I was overtaken by the night?
Not in the grotto that returns
the echo of my cry?

Oh no. To see him again—
it would not matter where—
in heaven's deadwater
or inside the boiling vortex,
under serene moons or in bloodless fright!

To be with him . . .
every springtime and winter,
united in one anguished knot
around his bloody neck!

TO THE CLOUDS

Ethereal clouds,
clouds like tulle,
transport my soul
through azure heaven.

Far from the house
that sees me suffer,
far from these walls
that watch me die!

Clouds of passage,
carry me to the sea
to listen to the song
of the high tide,
to sing amid
the flowering waves.

Clouds, blossoms, faces,
sketch me the one
who is gradually being erased
by time's infidelity.
My soul decays
without his face.

Clouds, passing
clouds, stop
over my heart
with your fresh mercy.
My lips are open:
I thirst.

SUMMIT

It is the afternoon hour,
the one that sets its blood
upon the mountains.

Someone in this hour
is suffering,
someone loses, anguished,
during this afternoon,
the only heart she pressed next to her.

Some heart lingers
where the afternoon soaks
that bloody summit.

The valley is already in shadows,
and is filling up with calmness.
But gaze up from the depths—
the mountain is blazing, red.

During this hour,
I always begin to sing
my invariable song of tribulation.
Could it be that I bathe
the summit scarlet?

I place my hand over my heart,
and I feel my side bleeding.

THE SLOW RAIN

This fainthearted and gloomy rain
like a suffering child,
before touching the Earth,
dies.

Quiet the tree, quiet the wind,
and within the stupendous silence
these fine, bitter tears
falling!

The sky is like an immense heart
that opens, bitter.
It is not raining: it is a slow
and long bloodletting.

Inside the house,
men don't feel this bitterness,
this shipment of sad water
from on high.

This long and weary descent
of conquered waters
to the prone, exhausted Earth.

It rains, and like a miserable jackal,
night lurks in the sierra.
What is going to surge
in the shadow of the Earth?

Will you sleep
while outdoors it falls,
suffering, this inert water,
this lethal water, sister of Death?

Tenderness

ROCKING

The divine sea rocks its
        endless waves.
Listening to the loving seas,
        I rock my child.

At night, the vagabond wind
        sways the wheat.
Listening to the loving winds,
        I rock my child.

The Heavenly Father silently rocks
        thousands of worlds.
Sensing His hand in the shadow,
        I rock my child.

CLOSE TO ME

Tender floss of my flesh
that I wove in my deep organs;
tender floss so easily chilled:
Sleep, close to me!

The partridge sleeps in clover,
listening to its heart beat.
Don't let my breathing disturb you:
Sleep, close to me!

Tiny, trembling herb
surprised by life
Don't leap from my breast:
Sleep, close to me!

I who have lost everything,
now shudder with thoughts of sleep.
Don't slip from my arms:
Sleep, close to me!

YOU HAD ME

Sleep, my child,
sleep smiling.
You are rocked
with a lullaby of stars.

You enjoyed the light
and were happy.
You had all goodness
when you had me.

Sleep, my child,
sleep smiling.
It is the loving Earth
that rocks you.

You beheld
the fiery crimson rose.
You reached out to the world,
you reached out to me.

Sleep, my child,
sleep, smiling.
It is God in the shadows
who rocks you.

THE SAD MOTHER

Sleep, sleep, my beloved,
without worry, without fear,
although my soul does not sleep,
although I do not rest.

Sleep, sleep, and in the night
may your whispers be softer
than a leaf of grass,
or the silken fleece of lambs.

May my flesh slumber in you,
my worry, my trembling.
In you, may my eyes close
and my heart sleep.

QUECHUAN SONG

The Indians were born
where Tihuantisuyo flourished.
They came to the puna
with dances, with hymns.

The quenas whistled;
two thousand live fires sizzled.
Golden Coyas
and blessed Amautas
offered their songs.

Blinded by suns,
you descended,
flying in your sleep,
to discover the widowed air
of the llama, of the Indian.

And where maize fields existed:
the wheat is rising.
In place of the vicuña,
young bulls run.

Return to your Pachacamac—
you've come in vain,
crazy Indian,
Indian who is born
a lost bird!

puna – acidic tableland
quenas – Quechua flute
Golden Coyas – Indian Queen
Amatuas – ceremonial poet and storyteller

CHILEAN EARTH

We dance on Chilean earth
more beautiful than Lia and Raquel:
the earth that kneads men,
their lips and hearts without bitterness.

The land most green with orchards,
the land most blond with grain,
the land most red with grapevines,
how sweetly it brushes our feet!

Its dust molded our cheeks,
its rivers, our laughter,
and it kisses our feet with a melody
that makes any mother sigh.

For the sake of its beauty,
we want to light up fields with song.
It is free,
and for freedom we want
to bathe its face in music.

Tomorrow we will open its rocks;
we will create vineyards and orchards;
tomorrow we will exalt its people.
Today we need only to dance!

ROUND OF COLORS

Wild blue and wild green,
from the branching, flowering flax,
seasick with the waves,
the comely blue one dances.

When blue sheds its leaves,
the green dancer follows:
clover green, olive green
and festive lemon green.

What beauty!
What color!

Gentle red and blood red
of rose and carnation—
when green grows weary,
it leaps into play like a champion.

They dance,
pitted against each other,
and who knows which is better.
The reds dance with so much fire.
They consume themselves with passion.

What caprice!
What color!

Yellow arrives
huge and full of fevers;
everyone makes way for it
as though bearing witness to Agamemnon.

For humanity and divinity,
the sacred splendor dances,
broadcasting golden aromas
and wings of saffron.

What delirium!
What color!

At last, they exit,
following the peacock sun
that picks them up
and carries them away
like a father or a thief.

Hand in hand with us,
they were, but are no longer:
the story of the world dies
when the storyteller gives up the ghost.

ROUND OF THE RAINBOW

for Freda Schultz de Montovani

Half of the round
was here and now it isn't.
The round was cut in half.

Come and wait for
a spectacle.
Half of the round
took off for the sky!

What celestial colors
come and go!
What skirts in the wind!
How beautifully they whirl!

From hill to hill, the rainbow dances
so that you will dance.
It might be playacting
or freewheeling,
never to return again.

We look to the sky and
all hues are here now:
half are crying,
the other half, laughing.

Oh, half of the wheel,
oh, come down, come down!
or bring us to all your colors
if by chance you won't drop down.

THOSE WHO DO NOT DANCE

An invalid girl asked,
"How do I dance?"
We told her:
let your heart dance.

Then the crippled girl asked,
"How do I sing?"
We told her:
let your heart sing.

A poor dead thistle asked,
"How do I dance?"
We told it,
let your heart fly in the wind.

God asked from on high,
"How do I come down from this blueness?"
We told Him:
come dance with us in the light.

The entire valley is dancing
in a chorus under the sun.
The hearts of those absent
return to ashes.

ARGENTINE ROUND

The round of Argentina
appears in the tropics
and going down the river
with its own rivers, it grows.
Plantations pass, they pass.
Cloaked in ferns, darkness comes.
We walk with the day,
and march on when night falls.

Leaving behind this Mesopotamia,
it shimmers and disappears.
The band is broken by the force of wheat.
Seven times we are torn apart,
seven times we are reunited.

Fat cattle cross the pampa.
A white round splits
into black and vermilion,
and with the wind of the pampa,
more songs grow.

Arriving in Patagonia,
white with ostriches,
we fish on islands
for the last fish.
The round of Argentina
appears in the tropics,
and the round reaches the place
where the world dies . . .

In the blanched Antarctic sea,
the sea tests its dregs,
and with a spin, it returns

to where the world dies:
the round of Argentina
appears in the tropics.

ROUND OF AROMAS

The sky's sweet basil,
fragrant mallow,
blue-fingered sage,
luxuriant anise.

They dance with passion
for the moon or the sun,
little heads, waists
and colors flying.

The wind tosses them,
heat opens them,
the river applauds them,
the drum enflames them.

When they were ordered
to become the aromatic leaf
they all spoke, "Yes!"
and shouted, "Me!"

Mint becomes a hasty bride,
taking the arm of the grand cedar,
and vanilla snares
the fragrant clove.

Let's dance feverishly,
wild with spice
Five weeks, five,
their splendor lasts.
And they never succumb to death,
only to love.

THE HOLLOW WALNUT

I

The rippled nut
with which you play,
fallen from the walnut tree,
did not bear witness to the Earth.

I found it in the pasture;
it didn't know who I was.
Cast from the sky,
the visionless one was ignorant
of its plight.
With it my possession,
I danced upon the green,
but it was deaf and did not hear
the horses running.

Don't disturb it.
A season of night lulls it to sleep.
When spring arrives,
you will split it open;
you will return it, unaware,
to God's world;
you will shout its name
and the name of the Earth.

II

But he split it open
without waiting,
and saw the dust fall
from the hollow walnut:
his hand filled

with dark death,
and he sobbed and sobbed
the entire night.

III

Let's bury it
under the grass
before spring comes.
Perhaps, in passing,
the God of life
will see it,
and with His hands touch
the Earth's dead one.

THE LITTLE BOX FROM OLINALÁ

for Ema and Daniel Cossío

I

My little box
from Olinalá
is rosewood
and jacaranda.

When suddenly I
open it, it exudes
a Queen-of-Sheba
fragrance.

Oh tropical
whiff of cloves,
mahogany
and copal!

I place it here,
I leave it there,
it comes and goes
through corridors.

It boils
from Grecian frets
like a land of
figwood, deer
and quail,

volcanoes
with great apertures
and the Indian

swaying in the wind
like corn.

Like so,
they are painted,
like so, like so:
Indian fingers
or hummingbirds;

and thus it is
made perfectly
by the Aztec hand,
the Quetzal hand.

II

When night
is about to fall,
because it guards me
from evil,

I place it on a
small pillow
where others place
their treasures.

It fills my dreams
with beauty.
It makes me laugh
and weep . . .

Through my hands,
the sea passes,
twin sierras,
furrowed fields.

One sees the Anahuac
shining again,
the beast of Ajusco
about to leap,

and through the path
that leads to the sea
Quetzalcoatl
will be reached.

It is my breath,
I am its feet;
it is knowledge;
I am delirium.

And we stop
like manna
where the road
is already abundant,

where they shout
to us *halala!*
The ladies of Olinalá.

box from Olinalá – boxes from Olinalá Mexico, made of fragrant wood, are
painted and decorated.
twin sierras – the East and West Sierra Madres
Ajusco – the hill Ajusco dominates the capitol.

THE RAT

A rat ran to a deer,
and the deer to a jaguar,
and the jaguar to the buffalo,
and the buffalo to the sea.

Seize, seize those who run away!
seize the rat, seize the deer,
seize the buffalo and the sea!

Look at the ringleader rat
carrying embroidery wool in its paws—
with that wool
I am decorating my dress,
and in that dress, I will marry.

Rise and make a path across the plain,
run breathlessly, without rest.
Fly for the sake of the fiancee and her beau,
and for her chariot and the wedding veil.

THE PEACOCK

The wind blew and carried the clouds
and upon the clouds a peacock vanished.
The peacock was destined for my hand,
the hand that will wither,
the hand that I gave this morning
to the king who came to marry.

Woe to the sky,
woe to the wind and to the clouds
that vanish with the peacock!

THE PARROT

The green and yellow parrot,
the green and saffron parrot,
called me "ugly" with its twangy voice
and satanic beak.

I am not ugly, because if I were ugly,
then ugly is my mother who looks like the sun,
ugly is the light my mother looks into,
and ugly is the wind that carries her voice,
and ugly is the water into which she falls
and ugly is the world and He who nurtured it.

The green and yellow parrot,
the green and sunflower parrot
called me "ugly" because it had not eaten,
and I bring it bread with wine,
but I am already tired of gazing at it,
always hanging on, always a sunflower.

THE AIR

This thing that passes and remains,
it is air—it is the air.
And without a mouth that you can see,
it takes you and kisses you, Father Lover.
Oh! We break it apart without breaking it;
wounded, it flies off without complaint.
And it seems that the Air
transports and leaves all behind, willingly.

FRUIT

In the white pasture of the sun,
fruit spills like chunks of gold.

The gold comes from Brazilian lands,
from the willowy darkness of Brazil's serenade.
My child, they send a clustered afternoon slumber.
I allow the glorious abundance to roll:
colors wheel with fragrance.

Crawling, you pursue the fruits
as though they were little girls,
scattering in all directions:
melting loquats
and hard, tattooed pineapples . . .

And all the things exude the aroma of Brazil,
breast of the world which they suckled.
Although not enjoying Atlantic water,
nevertheless, they could overflow its skirt.

Touch them, kiss them, whirl them,
and learn their faces.
Dream, child, that your mother
has ripened features;
the night is a black basket
and that the Milky Way is an orchard.

THE WILD STRAWBERRY

The wild strawberry, set apart
in a leafy tent,
gives off fragrance before she is picked.
Before she is seen, she blushes . . .
Untouched by birds,
it is heaven's dew
that moistens the wild strawberry.

Do not bruise the earth;
do not squeeze the sweet one.
For her love, lower yourself,
inhale her, and give her your mouth.

PINE FOREST

Let us go now into the forest.
Trees will pass by your face,
and I will stop and offer you to them,
but they cannot bend down.
The night watches over its creatures,
except for the pine trees that never change:
the old wounded springs that spring
blessed gum, eternal afternoons.
If they could, the trees would lift you
and carry you from valley to valley,
and you would pass from arm to arm,
a child running
from father to father.

HEAVEN'S CARRIAGE

Throw your head back, child,
and receive the stars.
At first sight,
they all sting and chill you,
and then the sky rocks
like a cradle that they balance,
and at a loss, you give up,
like something carried away and away.

God touches down to take us
into the nebula of his life;
he falls into the star-filled sky
like a waterfall set free.
Descend, descend into Heaven's Carriage.
It is going to arrive and it never does . . .

It comes down incessantly
and stops halfway
for love and the fear of love
that breaks or blinds us.
While it is en route,
we rejoice
and we cry when it leaves.

And one day the carriage doesn't stop.
It continues to descend and draws you near,
and you feel the live wheel—
the fresh wheel touches your heart.
Then rise without fear,
with a single leap to the wheel,
singing and crying exultantly
with the One who takes you and carries you away!

LADY SPRING

Lady Spring
is exquisitely dressed,
enrobed in lemon trees
and orange buds.

Her sandals are wide leaves,
and blushing fuchsias
complete her caravan.

Go out to meet her
along these roads.
She rides with sunshine
and trilled melodies.

Lady Spring,
with luxuriant breath,
laughs at all the world's pains.

She does not believe the one
who tells her about shattered lives.
How can she chance to touch
them among the sweet jasmine?

How can she discover them
reflected in fountains
of looking glass gold
and radiant songs?

From brown cracks
in the sick earth,
rose bushes light up
with red pirouettes.

She puts on her laces,
adorns herself green
over the somber stones
of the dead.

Lady Spring,
with your glorious hands,
make us, in the name of life,
scatter roses:

roses of joy,
roses of forgiveness,
roses of love
and exultation.

GUARDIAN ANGEL

It is the truth, not a fairytale:
there is a Guardian Angel
who takes you and carries you
like the wind
and follows children wherever they go.

He has soft hair
that flutters in the breeze,
sweet and serious eyes
that calm you with a glance,
killing fears and conjuring light.
(This is not a fairytale. It is true.)

He has a body, hands and winged feet,
six wings to fly or glide;
and these six wings
carry you through whirlwinds,
and likewise, shuttle you off to sleep.

He makes sweeter the ripe pulp
that your honey-fed lips crush;
he cracks the nut's sly shell,
and it is he who frees you
from gnomes and witches.

He helps you snip roses
seated in thorny traps;
he is the one who eases your way
through dangerous waters,
the one who helps you climb
prickly pine hills.

And although he walks along with you
making a pair,
a sweet cherry and its vermilion twin,
when with his sign, he places upon you
the gauge of sin,
he picks up your soul, leaving the body behind.

It is the truth, not a fairytale:
there is a Guardian Angel
who takes you and carries you
like the wind
and follows children wherever they go.

FOR NOEL

Father Christmas,
one with the prodigy's night,
Father Christmas,
with that great beard,
Father Christmas,
you come with delicate surprises
and secret, silent footsteps!

Tonight I am leaving you my stocking
hanging from the windowsill.
Don't empty all your sacks,
before you pass by my house.

Father Christmas, Father Christmas,
you're going to find my stockings
drenched with dew.
With rascal eyes, I've glimpsed
the river of your beard . . .

Shake out the tears and leave
each shoe brimming and stuffed full
with Cinderella's ring
and Red Riding Hood's wolf.

And don't forget Marta.
Her shoe is empty, too.
She is my neighbor
and I have cared for her
ever since her mama died.

Father Christmas,
old Father Christmas,
oh those huge hands spilling gifts,
those impish heaven-colored eyes

and that beard of wondrous fluff!

MOTHER POMEGRANATE

(based on a ceramic plate from Chapelle-aux-Pots)

I'll tell you a story in majolica;
purplish red and red come alive
in my majolica, the tale
of Mother Pomegranate.

Mother Pomegranate is old
and toasty like a French roll,
but her faithful crown consoles her,
the insatiable bounty of her tree.

Her deep house is divided
by slim lakes
where her children caper in ships
dressed in red, in scarlet.

With red passion, she adorns them,
using the same chasuble-skin;
and to prevent fatigue, Mother Pomegranate
never names or counts her seeds.

The overcrowded one
leaves her door ajar,
and the hemmed-in multitude breaks free;
she grew weary of sustaining their mansion.

And the children
of the purple one run away.
Mother Pomegranate remains
slumbering, empty . . .

They go off like ants,

extending themselves in threads,
equal, equal, equal,
a scarlet river of choirboys.

They arrive at the solemn cathedral,
and open the great iron door;
the babes of Mother Pomegranate
file in like tiny lobsters.

In the cathedral,
there are as many naves
as chambers in the pomegranate;
the choirboys come and go
in great waves of discovery.

A ruddy cardinal recites his work
with his back turned, armadillo-like.
A million choirboys incline
and rise to a voice.

The red stained glass windows
gaze back at them from high above,
with vivacious eyes,
like thirty red pheasants
with surprised hearts.

Bells begin to fly,
awakening the entire tiny valley;
they sound like red and garnet—
a castle on fire.

In chaos, the babes zoom
to the scandal of bronze;
they leap down onto the avenue
which appears stained with blood.

The city sleeps late,
and the poor one knows nothing;
the children abandon the streets
and with laughter return
to the country.

They arrive at her trunk,
quietly climb
and enter Mother Pomegranate's compartment;
in her they remain still
as the Stone of Kaaba.

Mother Pomegranate wakes up brimming,
plump with her simple red million;
she checks her balance for safety's sake,
and taps her pregnant pocket.

And Mother Pomegranate begins counting
and continues wondrously counting;
the children erupt in laughter
and she splits open with their guffaws.

The pomegranate split open
in the orchard
is a complete feast of fire;
we slice her and keep
the heart of hearts under her crown.

We place her on a white plate;
her blush of dreams
sounds an alarm.
Now I've told her story,
in shades of red,
in scarlet.

majolica - a type of ceramic

Felling of Trees

RICHES

I have an abiding bliss
and a lost fortune,
one like a rose,
the other like a thorn.
I was not cut off from that
which was stolen from me:
I have an abiding bliss
and a lost fortune,
and I am rich with purple
and with melancholy.
Oh, how beloved is the rose,
and what a lover, the thorn!
Like the double contour
of twin fruits,
I have an abiding bliss
and a lost fortune.

PARADISE

An engraving of expansive gold,
and upon the gilded flatlands,
two bodies like small golden threads.

A glorious body that hears
and a glorious body that speaks
in a meadow where nothing speaks.

A breath that seeks another breath
and a face that trembles because of this
in a meadow where nothing trembles.

Remember the sorrowful past
when they both had time
and lived afflicted,

until the hour of the golden spike
when time persisted at their doorstep
like homeless dogs.

GRACE

to Amado Alonso

A dappled bird,
a bird like jasper
went rainbow
wild
through the carriage
of the air.

This same early
morning,
the river passed by
like a lance.
The pure and clear
aurora remained
dazzling
with the wind's perfume.

Those who did not behold it,
don't know a thing.
They slept with tight sheets,
but I rose with shimmers of Venus—
half was evening,
half dawn.

The air tossed me
when she passed,
cruising by
like a wind and scintillation,
buffeting my face
and shoulders.

She seemed like a lily

or a swordfish.
Deep air shot free; she was
devoured by
the sprawling sky
and in an instant
vanished.
I remained trembling
on uncertain ground,
my good news
swept away!

THE ROSE

The richness at the center of a rose
is the richness of your heart.
Unfurl it as she does:
her girded boundary is all your affliction.

Set her free in song
or in great love.
Do not shield the rose:
she would burn you with her brilliance!

THE AIR FLOWER

for Consuelo Saleva

It was by fate that I found her
on foot in the middle of a meadow,
ruling over the passing world,
all who spoke to her
or beheld her presence.

And she said to me:
"Climb the mountain.
I never leave the meadow.
Cut the snow white flowers,
the tough and tender ones;
make them mine."

I climbed the bitter mountain,
and searched for where
flowers bloomed white among the rocks
in dreamy wakefulness.

When I came down with my heavy bouquet,
I found her at the meadow's heart,
and covered her feverishly
with a torrent of lilies.

And never witnessing their whiteness,
she said to me: "Now carry down
only red flowers.
Make them mine.
I cannot leave the meadow."

Along with the deer, I scaled rocks
and searched for mad flowers,

those that blush fevers and seem
to live and die of redness.

When I came down,
I offered my gift,
trembling and happy,
and she became like water
bloodied by the wounded deer.

But gazing at me,
awake in her dreams,
she said, "Go up and carry down
the yellow ones, the yellow ones.
I never leave the meadow."

Immediately, I climbed the mountain
and searched for thick buds
colored by sun and saffron,
newborn and already eternal.

When I found her, as always,
in the middle of the meadow,
I began showering her,
a second time,
and left her sparkling,
a garden of gold.

And still, intoxicated with
the yellow shine,
she told me: "Ascend, my servant,
and cut the colorless flowers,
not the saffron, not the vermilion.
The ones that I love grow
from memories of Eleanora and Ligeia;
they are colored like sleep and dreams.

I am the Lady of the Meadow."

I went off to conquer the mountain,
now black as Medea,
without a trace of brilliance;
it was like a grotto,
shadowy and certain.

They did not appear on branches;
they did not open their petals
among stones.
I cut them from the sweet air,
with scissors of love.

I clipped the blossoms
like a blind cutter.
I cut one air,
and then another;
the air became my jungle.

When I came down from the mountain,
and set off to find the Queen,
she now walked freely,
no longer white
or the color of violence.

The sleepwalker passed by,
abandoning the meadow,
and I followed her, following her,
through the pastures and poplar groves . . .

And with the garland of my treasure,
airy shoulders and hands,
I continue clipping bouquets from the air
and the air is my harvest . . .

She travels ahead, faceless,
she travels without a vestige,
and I still follow her
through a fog that branches

with these colorless buds,
not frost-white, not vermilion,
until I surrender to limitation,
when my time dissolves . . .

Mistral said of this poem, "I wanted to call this 'The Adventure,' my adventure with
poetry."

CARIBBEAN SEA

for A.E. Ribera Chevremont

Island of Puerto Rico,
island of palms,
light body, light,
like a saint,
lightly resting
over the water,
a thousand palm trees,
like the tallest—
from two thousand hills beckoning . . .

Island, sunrise of my joy,
without a body's affliction,
a tremulous soul,
nursed by constellations
in the siesta of fire,
perforated by dialects,
and maiden-like again in the innocent dawn.

Passionate island
of sugarcane and coffee:
a world sweet on the lips
like childhood,
blessed with song
like a Hosanna!
Songless siren
over the sea,
offended by the sea
in the surf:
Cordelia of the waves,
bitter Cordelia.

Save yourself
like the white roe deer,
and like the new llama
of Pachacamac,
and like the golden egg
of the brood,
and like Ifigenia
alive in the flames?
May the archangels
of our race
save you:
Michael, the avenger;
Raphael, the foot soldier;
and Gabriel, our conductor
to the last hour.

Before my feet
and vision fail me,
before my skin becomes a fable,
before my knees
fly in the wind . . .

Philippine Independence Day

Cordelia – King Lear's honest daughter.
Pachacamac – supreme Quechua god

THE FOREIGN WOMAN

to Francis de Miomandre

She speaks with abandonment
about her savage seas
of mystic algae and sands.
She prays to God without burden or bulk.
This woman is ancient and ready to die.
She has made our garden otherworldly,
cultivating cactuses and herbs
that rustle in the wind like sails.
She breathes the desert's exhalation
and has loved with a white-hot passion:
her secret, if unveiled,
would be like the map of another star.
For eighty years she will live among us,
but it will always seem as though
she has just arrived,
speaking a language of shivers and groans
that only elvish animals understand.
And she will die surrounded by us
during a night of supreme suffering,
with only her destiny for a pillow:
a quiet and foreign death.

REFRESHMENT

to Dr. Pedro de Alsa

I recall the gestures
of children
and they are gestures of water offerings.

In the valley of the Río Blanco
where the Aconcagua is born,
I went to drink, leapt with thirst
into the frothy spume of a waterfall
that fell long-haired and hard
and broke, tense and white.
I pressed my mouth to the bubbling cascade,
and the holy water burned me;
for three days my mouth bled
because of that taste of Aconcagua.

In the open country of Mitla,
a day full of grasshoppers,
of sun, of walking,
I knelt at a well;
an Indian came to hold me over the water;
my head, like a fruit,
was nestled in his palms.
I drank what he drank;
it was his face against my face,
and as lightning shone I realized
the flesh of Mitla was my caste.

On the island of Puerto Rico,
during the sparkling blue siesta,
my still body, the crazy waves,
and with hands clapping

like a hundred mothers,
there came a little girl of grace;
next to my mouth she put
a coconut shell brimming with water,
and I drank it, like a child,
maternal water, water from her hands.
And my thirst has never been quenched
with greater sweetness in body or soul.

In my childhood home,
my mother used to bring me water.
Between sips, I glimpsed her above the jar.
Her head rose to me;
the jar came further down.
I still possess that valley;
I keep my thirst and her face.
This is probably eternity:
that we are still as we were.

I recall the gestures
of children
and they are gestures of water offerings.

THINGS

for Max Daireaux

I love the things I never had,
along with others
that I no longer possess.

I touch the silent water,
still in cold pastures;
without the wind
it used to shiver
in the orchard that was my orchard.

I look at it
as I used to look at it;
it gives me strange thoughts,
and I play slowly with this water
as with a fish or a mystery.

I think about the threshold where
I left behind happy footsteps
now foreign to me,
and on this threshold I see a wound
full of moss and silence.

I'm searching for a poem that I've lost.
It was told to me at the age of seven.
She was a woman baking bread
and I can still see her saintly mouth.

A broken aroma comes in the wind.
I'm very lucky if I sense it.
It is a slender and tenuous aroma,

the perfume of almond trees.

My senses become children;
I seek a name for this
and don't get it right,
and I inhale the air and places,
looking for almond trees
but I don't find them.

Nearby a river always sounds.
For forty years it has been my intuition.
It is my blood's exercise in song
or a rhythm that I was given.

Or it is the Elquí River of my childhood
in which I travel upstream and wade.
I never lose this place.
Our hearts are united
like two children;
we have each other.

When I dream of the cordillera,
I walk through slim passageways,
and continue hearing,
without a pause for mercy,
a whistling, almost a curse.

I see to the edge of the Pacific,
my pale archipelago,
and from an island
a bitter smell of the dead halcyon
clings to me.

A spine, a grave and sweet spine,
ends the dream that I dream.

It is the end of my road
and I rest when I arrive.

Is it a dead tree trunk or my father,
this vague spine of ashes?
I don't ask, I don't disturb it.
I lie down with it in silence and sleep.

I love a stone from Oaxaca
or Guatemala, and move closer to it:
red and fixed like my face
with a crack for breath.

When I fall asleep, it remains naked;
I don't know why I overturn it.
And maybe I never possessed it—
it is my tomb that I see.

WALL

Simple and extraordinary wall.
wall without weight and without color:
a hint of air in the air.

From a hillside, birds pass,
light passes like a swing,
the edge of winter passes
like a breath of summer.
A leafy wind
and embodied shadows pass.

But a sigh does not break bounds,
arms do not meet,
and no heart-to-heart is made flesh.

SONG OF THE DEAD GIRLS

for my niece Graciela

And what ever happened
to the poor dead girls
so cleverly kidnapped
from their April days,
those who rose and submerged
like dolphins in the waves?

Where did they go,
and where are they found?
Were they trapped with knives of laughter
or seized while awaiting
the voice of a lover in pursuit?

Were they erased like sketches
that God did not want to color again
or drowned little by little,
like a garden flooded by its fountains?

At times they long
to trace their profiles in water,
and among the flesh-red roses,
their smiles are almost seen.

Their bodies and shadows
become fleeting visions in pastures;
through enchantment, they almost
convince a cloud to lend them shape.

They almost mend their broken bodies;
they almost arrive happy at the sun;
they almost disown their cursed road

and remember their way back home.

They almost defeat their betrayal
and walk back to the fold.
And in the afternoon
we can almost see
the divine million come!

CONFESSION

I

It hangs from the edges of your mouth—
your confession hangs and I see it;
it almost drops into my hands.

Confess, man of sins,
saddened by your transgression,
without a happy gait,
without your poplar-tree voice,
far away from the ones you love,
because your crime does not wound
as much as its fruit.

Your mother is younger than
the one who listens to you,
and your son is so tender
that you will burn him like a fern
if your sins are revealed.

I am old as stone to hear you,
as deep as forty years of moss to hear you;
my face lacks amazement or anger,
carrying charity from many lifetimes ago,
to hear you.

Give me the years
that you might want to give me;
they are less than have been left
upon these sands by others;
they did not speak in vain,
and mercy ages like tears

and swells the heart just as wind
swells the dunes.

Confess so that I may depart with it
and leave you pure.
Never again will you see the same woman
that you now behold;
nor will you hear this voice that answers you.
Rather, you will grow lighthearted as before,
descending slopes or climbing hills,
and you will again kiss without affliction,
and play with your son on stones of gold.

II

Now you are growing new shoots
and living new days;
may the sea's iodine help you.
You no longer sing the tunes
that you once knew;
you do not lie about the villages, valleys,
and their creatures once known to you.
Be again the dolphin and good petrel
enraptured by the sea and solid ship.

But one day, sit upon another dune,
in the sunshine, as when you found me,
when your son is thirty years old,
and listen for the other who comes,
the edges of his mouth burdened
as though with algae,
and with your head bowed, ask him also,
and later don't ask, but rather listen

for three days and three nights,
and receive the blame,
like clothing made unbearably heavy
with sweat and shame—
beg forgiveness on your two knees!

CATALONIAN WOMEN

"Perhaps the epithalamic sea beckons
and calls for virgins;
perhaps we are all the one
who used to be called Nausicaa."

"We kiss better along the dunes
than under the thresholds of houses,
testing the mouth and offering the mouth
with bitter and sweet almonds."

"Pruners of olive trees,
grinders of almond milk,
we descend from Montserrat
to embrace the surf."

THE ESCAPE

Dear Mother, in a dream
I cross livid landscapes,
a black mountain that always
twists to reach the other mountain,
where you continue to remain vaguely,
but there always is another round mountain
to encompass, to pay the passage
to the mountain of your pleasure,
of my pleasure.

But, at intervals, you proceed making
a road of deceptions and of spoils.
We two journey sensing each other,
knowing each other,
but we cannot see each other in the eyes,
and we cannot exchange words,
like Eurydice and Orpheus alone,
the two fulfilling an oath or punishment,
both with broken feet and accent.

But at times, you are not at my side:
I carry you inside of me, an anguished
and loving weight, and at the same time;
I am like a child galley slave
with his father galley slave,
and it is necessary to string together
the repetitious hills,
without revealing the painful secret:
that I am carrying you away,
stolen from the cruel gods,
we go forward to a God that belongs to us.

And at other times,

you are not on the hill straight ahead.
You don't go away with me.
You don't flee in my breath.
You have dissolved in the fog of the mountains.
You have given into the livid landscape.
You respond to me with a sarcastic voice,
from three points, and in pain, I am shattered,
because my body is one,
that which you gave me,
and you are water with a hundred eyes,
and you the thousand-armed countryside,
never again to be what the beloved are:
one live heart over another live heart,
a bronze knot softened by tears.
And we never are, we never remain
as they say the glorious ones remain,
before their God, in two rings of light
or in two amazed medallions,
joined together in a glorious ray
or lying in sleep on a golden riverbed.

Oh I search for you
and you don't know that I am searching for you,
or you go with me, and I don't see your face;
or you go off within me because of a terrible pact,
without responding to me with your deaf body,
always through the rosary of hills
that charge blood to give pleasure;
they make each one dance in turn,
until the moment of the burning temples,
of old insanity's rattlesnake,
and the trap in the red vortex!

Wine Press

THE OTHER

I killed someone
inside of me.
I didn't love her.

She was a fiery flower
of the mountain cactus;
she was thirst and flames,
never stopping for refreshment.

She traveled a rocky way,
and pressed her shoulders against the sky;
she never descended
to search for *the eyes of water.*

The grass withered
where she rested,
burned by her breath
and face of incandescent coals.

With rapid resins,
her speech hardened
never to be set free
in a glorious cascade.

This mountain flower
did not know how to bend—
but by her side,
I bent.

I allowed her to die,
robbing her of my heart.
She perished like an eagle
left to starve.

The thunder in her wings
became silent;
she fell and withered
in my hands,
final embers . . .

Her sisters still cry out
to me for her sake,
and a clay fire
claws me in passage.

As I travel,
I tell them:
Look through the ruins
and with the clay create
another eagle with wings of fire.

If you cannot, then,
oh! Forget her.
I killed her.
You must kill her, too!

CALIFORNIA POPPY

to Eda Ramuli

Flame of California,
hardly tall as a hand,
tongues of gold return,
you lap the beech-lined avenues:
unlike an ordinary poppy,
you carry the hue of spilled honey.

Prodigal wisps,
a few weeks of treasure,
and the little you bring
is equal to the soul,
a brilliant testimony to help
raise our prayer of thanksgiving.

In the palm, you quickly wither,
shrinking from the touch;
your four rapid words
are like swallowed lips
when they break your spine,
unable to fathom your heavenly
hymn of praise.

Passion of California,
sharp call, you give off
four puffs of fire
along an innocent highway,
and it is a mystery
for whom you journey or stop.

The frenetic route runs
like a Fury set free,

and you desire salvation,
your shoulders are strong,
amber feeding the sand,
the stuff of California.

Sharing the air of tall
orange and apple trees,
you do not blink at hunger
or thirst: you only sing adoration
with four live tongues
and a throat of flame.

Your worship breaks the day,
especially the siesta,
and with the afternoon askew,
with dazzling looks,
your daughters now take over
the five senses,
to dance and chant exaltation.

What are you there in the place you inhabit?
Are you tall and enchanted?
And from where did you descend,
condensing joy and flame?
How complete you were above us
without a wintry plan!

Your poor glory and mine
(your poor soul, my poor soul),
we burn without provocation,
and are equally urged to touch
this shore of the world,
descendants of Our Flame!

A REQUEST FOR BLANCA

for Blanca Subercaseaux

I don't know
if I'll be able to visit.
We'll see
if I can fulfill your wish, Sister.

If I come, I'll arrive
wrapped in sweet air;
I'll not bring ice to your level land.
Or I'll visit the sharp edges
of your dreams with love,
without words.

Rise up if I cannot make it
and we will meet half way,
and bring me a bit of earth
to remind me of my home.

Don't be afraid
if I come without baggage,
if I arrive in silence.
And don't cry if
I bring you no answers.
My sin was the word.
But give me yours, yours—
it was like a dove resting,
at home.

DAWN

I expand my heart so that
like a cascade of fire
the Universe may enter.
The new day arrives and its coming
leaves me breathless.
I sing like a high-crowned grotto.
I sing my new day.

Because of the loss of grace
I have lost and found,
I am humble;
without offering,
without receiving,
until night's Gorgon
turns away, defeated,
on the run.

MORNING

She has returned, she has returned.
Each morning the same yet new.
Anticipated yesterday
and forever,
she must arrive this morning.

Empty-handed morning
that promised and cheated.
Behold another morning unfurl,
leap like the deer of the East,
awake, jubilant and new,
alive, brisk, and rich with work.

Brother, raise your head
from your chest
and receive her.
Make yourself worthy
of the one that leaps skyward,
and like a halcyon,
pushes off and rises,
a golden halcyon,
swooping down to us with songs.
Hallelujah, Hallelujah, Hallelujah!

DUSK

I feel my heart melt
like candles in the sweetness:
an oil of langour,
not wine,
fills my veins.

And I feel my days fleeing,
silent and gentle as a gazelle.

NIGHT

Mountains vanish,
cattle wander
and are lost;
the sun returns to its forge:
everyone has fled.

Fields are being erased,
the granary has sunk,
and my cordillera depresses
its summit and live lamentation.

Animals stray, slanting
toward forgetfulness.
And the two of us also spin our way
into the night, my child.

THE CHRISTMAS STAR

A little girl
comes running,
she caught and carries a star.
She goes flying, making the plants
and animals she passes
bend with fire.

Her hands already sizzle,
she tires, wavers, stumbles,
and falls headlong,
but she gets right up with it again.

Her hands don't burn away,
nor does the star break apart,
although her face, arms,
chest and hair are on fire.

She burns down to her waist.
People shout at her
and she won't let it go;
her hands are parboiled,
but she won't release the star.

Oh how she sows its seeds
as it hums and flies.
They try to take it away—
but how can she live
without her star?

It didn't simply fall—it didn't.
It remained without her,
and now she runs without a body,
changed, transformed into ashes.

The road catches fire
and our braids burn,
and now we all receive her
because the entire Earth is burning.

MY MOTHER

I

My mother was very small
like mint or grass;
she hardly cast a shadow
over things, hardly,
and the Earth loved her
when it felt her lightness
and because she smiled upon it
in happiness and in pain.

Children loved her,
and the old ones, and the grass,
and the light that loves grace—
it searched for her and wooed her.

Because of her, perhaps this love
doesn't rise up: that which without
a whisper walks and silently speaks:
the grassy horizon
and the spirit of water.

To whom am I telling this
from a foreign land?
In the mornings I speak this way of her
so that they will resemble her,
and along my interminable route,
I march on speaking to the Earth.

And when a far off voice
comes singing and arrives;
I follow it like a lost soul
and wander without finding it.

Why was she taken so far away
so that I cannot reach her?
And if she always helped me,
why doesn't she respond, descend?

Who carries away her body now?
I will go out to find her.
She walks so far away
that her sharp voice doesn't reach me.
I rush through my days
like someone who hears a call.

This night that is full of you,
given over only to you,
take it, although you are timeless,
feel it, hear it, reach it.
Nothing remains of this day's end
but hope and anxiety.

II

Something comes from far away,
something is present,
something comes forward;
without a body or a whisper it comes,
but the arrival never ends.
Although it truly comes,
why does it walk on and not reach me?

It is you who walks lightly,
with steps of caution.
Arrive, arrive, arrive at last,
most faithful and most beloved.
What do you need where you dwell?

Is it your river, your mountain?
Or am I the one, who without understanding
creates the delay?
The Earth and sea don't hold me
like your song;
the dawn and dying sunsets
do not conquer me.

The earth does not hold me;
nor the sea rhat sings like you;
I am not enthralled by the dawn
or dying sunsets.

I am alone with the night,
the Great Bear, the Balance,
believing that through this peace
your word can travel,
my breath breaking it,
my cry, driving it away.

Come, mother, come, arrive,
without knocking.
Accept the vision and sound
of this forgotten night
in which we remain orphans
without a destination, without a watchful eye.

It is a suffering like jagged stones,
frost and the rough surf.
For the love of your daughter,
agree to listen to the owl and the waves,
but don't go back without
taking me home with you.

III

So arrive, give me your face,
a word in the wind.
And if you don't take me away,
stay tonight. Don't go.
Although you will not answer me,
everything tonight is a word:
a face, the wind, the silence,
and the boiling Milky Way.

So . . . so . . . more still . . .
Stay, morning has not come,
and night has not closed.
Time grows thin,
the two to be equalled,
and quiet returns,
a slow passage to the homeland.

IV

It must be this, Mother, speak,
eternity has arrived,
days are ending,
and it is a century of nothingness,
between life and death,
without desire, the darkness.
What is there then if not
delays, changes?

What was this? How did it happen?
How does it incessantly endure?
I don't want to demand;
I proceed understanding, frightened,
tearful and babbling

the words that you gave me,
said to me, which melt into one passionate:
Thank You.

WHAT DO YOU FEEL UNDERGROUND?

Underground do you feel
the delicate warmth of this spring?
Does the sharp perfume of honeysuckle
reach you through the earth?

Do you remember the sky,
the clear jets of mountain water,
the shimmering summit?
Do you remember the deep-tapestried path,
my still hand in your trembling hand?

This spring perfumes and refines
the sweet liquor of veins.
If only underground your beautiful
closed mouth could savor it!

Bordering the river, to this green
redolence you would come.
You might like the ambivalent warmth
of my mouth, its soft violence.

But you are underground—
your tongue silenced by dust;
there is no way that you can sing with me
the sweet and fiery songs of this spring.

SONNETS OF DEATH (V)

I chose among others, proud and glorious,
this destiny, a bygone vocation of tenderness,
a bit reckless, a bit shadowy,
to become a wreath of mustard over his tomb.

Men pass by. They pass with mouths expressing
a happy and forever renewed song
that now is lusty, and tomorrow, crazy,
and later, mystical. I chose this invariable

song with which I lull to sleep a dead man
who was distant from all reality, and in all dreams, mine:
he who enjoyed other lips, and rested upon another woman's
breast,

but at this time, so exact and long,
only these servant lips of humble mustard
sing him to sleep in sweetness over this bitter earth.

Poem of Chile

VALPARAÍSO

Valparaíso is fading,
winking with its sailboats
and bannered ships
that call us to embark.
But sirens do not count
with these adventurers.

CLOVER PATCH

A whistling from Aconcagua
reaches me and carries me away again.
There is a highland in clover
with velvet touches
where it waits, broken,
and stopped, as though fenced in:
the round we began
between Earth and Heaven.

If I go,
I enter and give my hand.
Again, it begins to whirl,
but the one who shouted it,
no longer gives his voice.
He is motionless.

The man referred to in the second stanza was the President of Chile, Don
Pedro Aguirre Cerda.

THE POPLAR TREES

The poplar trees follow us
and carry us without knowing it
through their open green sheath,
singing their palpitations,
laughing, joyously laughing,
with laughter that is mirth,
with their ecstatic trunks
and their arms in flight . . .

The slow and unwound one
carries us, with inner magic,
like the archangel Raphael
in an ineffable succession,
and the march gladdens us
with laughter and rattling bells.

To where are they guiding us
so that we might cross them
like a corridor of grace
that silences the march in flight?

TALCAHUANO

From Talcahuano comes
dockyard traffic.
The arsenals breathe heavily,
eating and casting off iron,
and bandaged skulls shine
with long steel
ribbons.

Angry ships enter,
and others leave erect.
They go to sea like
a tuna, caught and returned.
And the sea enters and departs,
plunging bluish, searching for
those it wants to win;
it hates at the same time
with charm and fetters:
a swindler's love.

CONCEPCIÓN

The wide and womanly city
does not yield herslef to the Philistine.
Soft is her breast of parks
and her streamy cap.
Visited by the Spirit,
she receives happiness and pain, alike,
and pine groves perfume
her joyful spirit and understanding.

If I arrive at midnight,
I have a place to rest my head,
and a table prepared for my comfort,
but travelling this way—
like a ghost—
I frighten the ones I love so well,
and upon the threshold,
they leave for me
my light ash-colored bundles.

THE MAYTEN

We will dream our siesta
where the moisture of dark,
dewy earth begins,
and the mayten springs to life.
Look at the mayten—See it.
Diaguita, of the thirsty lips.
In greenness, it is a beautiful bachelor,
in protection, a grandfather.
Like a liberated waterfall,
it delivers a green spectacle,
and during the siesta, it is more precious
than a larch or nut pine.

Look at the enchanted mayten,
baby son of the desert,
the little beast sprouts its tail,
spiralling . . .

The Mayten – an ornamental Chilean evergreen tree

Diaguita – a member of the Diaguita Indians of Argentina

Prose

In Praise of Earthly Things

THE SEA

Again the sea, the singing and eternally unrestrained sea, again its great light in my eyes and its gift of forgetfulness.

The sea washes away the past just as communion washes away misery from the believer; the sea bestows the only perfect freedom. From it comes a true state of grace, innocence, and happiness.

Man forgets his occupation and limitations; he lets the pain and the pleasure earth gives him fall like shameful things that discolor the sea and exist only on the earth's crust. Whatever part of him is circumstantial, whatever is a product of time and place—all breaks apart over the marvelous sea. We are only naked essence, man or woman, without another name or contingency. We are the body that loves iodine and salt—we were born for them. The eye delights over the horizon, and the ear receives rhythm. Nothing more.

It is a redemption that returns to be lost again—like the other: in port, redemption of the vile cities and inane actions, the dirty fabric of life, that which can sometimes be cut mercifully with a slash, letting it fall like an old tunic torn at the shoulders.

After a year on land, I now feel that life rots inside of me. It softens and grows lax like a fig fallen from a branch. Among human-fruits, I am a sea-fruit with a thirst for bitter sap, destined to be devoured by the albatross' bills.

Now the mountain seems to me a creature dehumanized by excellence; it has nothing in common with the flesh that rejects it. It holds onto its answers and secrets. Wild abandon exists under its skirts for the one who adores the world below. The sea stimulates words, and on good days it seems that its celebration was made for us . . .

But the journey, the true journey is not this one, or the one that the traveler, a master of crows, undertakes (the ownership of his life is not returned). It is not the mariner's voyage, a cause of worry for both the seashore and the woman. It is not my journey. The journey is one without a predestined port or destiny, without a date. It is a trip through the sea and for the sea, with no objective greater than the naked horizon and the eternally budding waves.

But this cannot be forced upon someone. It belongs to free souls, inhabitants of an uncharted planet. They have no greater objective in life than the experience of life itself: slowly coming to know and savor the elements with lungs and loving eyes.

THE BODY

What would the body of Saint Francis be like? They say it was so delicate that it might have disappeared in the wind. It cast very little shadow: one's shadow is like pride in earthly possessions, like the shadow of a tree painting the grass, or the shadow of a woman who passes through a fountain and is instantly drenched. The humble one hardly cast a shadow.

He was small in stature. Just like a whitecap crossing the water, he traveled and sensed the presence that watched over his body.

His arms were light, so light. He did not feel them at his sides when they dropped. His head was like the small stamen inside a flower.

He walked gracefully: his legs passed lightly over the grass without trampling it, and his chest was narrow, although wide for love (love is the essence and not water which requires great vessels!). And his shoulders . . . they were narrowed by humility; they made one think of a very small cross, one smaller than the other.

His sides were burned to a slenderness. The flesh of youth had vanished, along with its sins.

Perhaps his small body crackled, just as dry cactuses crackle with heat.

Human happiness is something like pregnancy; he did not want it. Pain is another thicket of conquests, and he fled from it. His heavenly pleasure and sustenance was the love of animals. He tended to see the world as a place as light as a flower. And he, resting within his own boundaries, did not want to weigh more than a nectar-seeking bee.

Who sings better in the valleys when the wind passes? Those with fat ears say it is the river that shatters goblets in the gravel; others say it is a woman who refines a cry in her fleshy throat.

But the best cry comes from the small, empty vehicle, where there are no inner organs for the voice to be hindered, and this small car, guided through the valleys, is you, little Francis, the one who has hardly made his mark on the world. You are like a small, slim shadow.

IN PRAISE OF GOLD

The slim flake of gold that I raised to my eyes and viewed against the light of May, made me look almost greenish, a twin tint which was halting, like my own, a shade between green and gold. It riveted me like the gaze of a twin brother.

Gold pounded to dust, returns pathetic-looking. Against the sun, it takes on a violet hue, and aspires to purple, because like other kings, such as David or Louis of Bavaria, it also wants to know anguish.

Gold offers flakes of coverage to a young girl, who exits the river without her clothes. The girl accepts the dry gauze of gold; it plays a colorful trick on her with its splendid shine. Later, she picks it up, leaf by leaf, and when, in her palm, she finishes the examination, she knows that the ornamentation she gathers is less heavy than an oily leaf. It remains in her hand, weighing less than a drop of blood.

The Golden One is used up with a touch; it is like the shame of being beautiful and unfinished, a shame that comes when comparing oneself with the divine; it consoles me when I think about my own death.

An old one called gold "sweet metal" when he viewed it alongside the stubborn types. It is the hardest, peerless pollen, or even a slightly harder wax.

Irritant-free gold (like the angelic ancients) is found among the sins of mud and acid.

Gold infuses the rivers I know. It makes lime sweeter; it carves aquatic lips, and longs for the heft of musical water over its face.

Gold voluntarily bonded with second son silver, showing

a Christian appetite for humility.

     The alchemist named gold using the sun's cipher for consolation. I reproach gold sparked and sustained by the sun; it must die with the other, blackening itself in bereavement, like cinders, because it is faithful. According to Boghes, an Arab with a universal message, all bodies pass through one last stage: some become almonds of gold, others become silver almonds. (This was told to me—I don't *want* to decompose.) Believing Boghes, here I leave my golden words. They might become my ultimate flesh, the surprise I face in this world.

THE LARK

You said that you loved the lark more than any other bird because of its straight flight toward the sun. That is how I wanted our flight to be.

Albatrosses fly over the sea, intoxicated by salt and iodine. They are like unfettered waves playing in the air, but they do not lose touch with the other waves.

Storks make long journeys; they cast shadows over the Earth's face. But like albatrosses, they fly horizontally, resting in the hills.

Only the lark leaps out of ruts like a live dart, and rises, swallowed by the heavens. Then the sky feels as though the Earth itself has risen. Heavy jungles below do not answer the lark. Mountains crucified over the flatlands do not answer.

But a winged arrow quickly shoots ahead, and it sings between the sun and the Earth. One does not know if the bird has come down from the sun or risen from the Earth. It exists between the two, like a flame. When it has serenaded the skies with its abundance, the exhausted lark lands in the wheatfield.

You, Francis, wanted us to achieve that vertical flight, without a zigzag, in order to arrive at that haven where we could rest in the light.

You wanted the morning air filled with arrows, with a multitude of carefree larks. Francis, with each morning song, you imagined that a net of golden larks floated between the Earth and the sky.

We are burdened, Francis. We cherish our lukewarm rut: our habits. We exalt ourselves in glory just as the towering grass aspires. The loftiest blade does not reach beyond the high pines.

Only when we die do we achieve that vertical flight! Never again, held back by earthly ruts, will our bodies inhibit our souls.

IN PRAISE OF SMALL TOWNS

Small towns possess humility—it is a natural characteristic. They are not caught up in lust for domination. Small towns are places where no one owns too much; therefore, in none of them does materialism become a dominant force.

Generally, they lack rudeness, and humility and modesty exist there, creating the intimate spaces we look at each day.

In order to get to know ourselves, we live with faces and breath in harmony. Happiness and pain are common to us. This brings men back to lullabies; the pulse of the first reaches the last. Therefore, it is not possible to ignore great misery, or remain in a cold trance when faced with a neighbor's tragedy.

(If such a thing happened, the selfish one would live pierced by the arrows of all eyes).

In these few towns, the first man and the last man have learned to form an effective brotherhood, elbows touching as much in serious comradeship as in the most pleasant diversions.

In the small land of neighbors, a variety of human professions abound: the shepherd, the farmhand, the farmer, the gardener, the bricklayer, the goldsmith, the sculptor, the ironworker, the weaver, the poet and the musician. All vocations come to life at the same time over five hundred or a thousand hectars of earth. This small land does not suffer famine.

Someone builds houses; someone assembles pieces of a watch. In the distance, someone makes the great choir sing. Each one has his place, and it is known, respected, and cherished by all.

IN PRAISE OF STONES

Kneeling stones, stones falling in cavalcades, and those never wanting to fall, like a heart become too weary.

Stones resting on their shoulders are like dead warriors—their wounds are sealed with pure silence, not with bandages.

Stones hold scattered gestures like lost children: an eyebrow on the sierra, an ankle in a stone bench.

Stones remember a unified face and want to piece it back together, gesture by gesture, someday.

Stones heavy with sleep, rich with dreams, like a peppercorn guarding pure essence, languid and drowsy, like a tree of conjunctures, stone savagely clutches its treasure of absolute dreams.

Kneeling stones, commingled stones, stones falling in cavalcades, and those not wanting to fall, like a heart become too weary.

The headstone destined for Jacob's neck, the stone of mourning is like a number— without a blush and without dew—it is just like a number.

Round stone is simply a great eyelid, with eyelashes, like Methuselah's. The hooked summit of the mystical Andes, that flame that doesn't dance, halted abruptly like Lot's wife Sarah. It did not want to answer me when I was a child, and it still does not answer me.

Stones flashing with gold or silver, suddenly pierced by copper, are startled by the intrusion. Stones are irritated by metallic almonds, as though they were invisible darts.

Kneeling stones, commingled stones, stones running in phalanxes or throngs, without arriving anywhere.

Ancient river stones from slippery shores are like the drowned—they hold the same withered vegetation that sticks fast to the hair of the drowned. But tender stones exist; they can touch someone who has been flayed and not hurt him. They pass over his body with a tongue like his own mother's, and they don't grow tired.

Young river stones are pebbles painted like fruit. Yes, they can sing! Once, when I was also five years old, I placed them under my pillow; they made a commotion like a mountain of tots being smothered, or perhaps they took turns singing a round at the nucleus of my dream. They were its masters: tender-aged pebbles came to my sheets and played with me.

Some stones do not want to become tombstones or fountains; they shun a foreign touch and refuse the intrusive inscription in order to make their own gestures, unique language, rise someday.

Mute stones, their hearts are bestowed with a passion that could be given away. In order not to disturb the slumber of their vertiginous almond—only for that reason, they remain still.

THE GIRAFFE

Other animals see her pass by and ask each other what heavenly thing is worthy of that high neck.

"She probably has better information about storms," the hares say.

"What a stupid hunger for horizons," comments the zebra, the giraffe's cousin in design. The zebra advises her to give back her body's line, although it may break her back.

Disproportion frightens the giraffe's own hind legs. It is believed that two giraffes exist: one, a relative of the ass, tall as God willed her to be—and the other, a bewitched specimen, aspiring to reach her nocturnal home.

"Stop it," the back legs say. "Don't go on!" She ventures ahead, exploring the forest, shouting at the tall trees: "Open up, open up!"

The noble, lazy trees do not lift their leaves. She passes by, opening great passageways, and she exits the forest, leaving it parted like cathedral naves.

She travels offering her services for great committees: one before the elephant who must shade the sunbaked farmland, and the other before the mill that does not allow a patch of moss to sleep. But the elephant and the mill do not trust the giraffe, and it seems a bad omen to listen to her.

It is said that the giraffe has two aspects: one good, and the other, twisted. She does not have a vocation, and only a band of Bedouins once employed her to raise their patchwork tent when its frame was broken. Since then, the giraffe continues her journey, dappled with big black flowers. The drunken Bedouins scribbled pictures on her, all night long!

My God, what is the giraffe?

The animal answers, telling me she is simply ugly because she resembles my own fractured passion.

AN OWL

She is completely white with an ancient headdress and amber talons. The beak belongs to an old Lady Macbeth, heavy with grief.

She is irritated by the day's leap to life, its hard-quartz brightness. Clarity is set free; the noise of the park has imitated Lady Macbeth's sanguinary eye.

"All those who pass by"—she tells me—"cannot understand the old white owl, her garnet eyes. They stop in front of me, quickly look at me, and move on to the cage of the frenetic parrots from Borneo. If they remained with me for a time, despite my sadness, I would tell them something about the night they ignore like a foreign land. The night is like a harvest of seven consecutive carcasses, and I have arrived at its empty purple almond. Night's almond is ineffable. It has softened my downy feathers and tapered my ears. I hear . . . I hear the wool bundle of the alpaca's neck, growing; I hear the horn of the black bison, hardening. I hear the high and attentive vein in your neck.

"Touch me. See if you can enjoy a thought cloistered in this silence. And when this night passes, see if you obtain a poem as soft as my oblique flight."

And I do not touch her. Despite her breast of fantasy and coagulated silence, I know her and tell her:

"You are the White Devil. You fly crookedly like the lightning I observed one night. My eye, also, turns red in vigilance."

THE ALPACA

She is harnessed for a long journey; on her back she carries an entire store of wool.

She walks without rest, and sees with eyes full of strangeness. The wool merchant has forgotten to come to get her, and she is ready.

In this world, nothing comes better equipped than the alpaca; one is more burdened with rags than the next. Her sky-high softness is such that if a newborn is placed on her back, he will not feel a bone of the animal.

The weather is very hot. Today, large scissors that will cut and cut represent mercy for the alpaca.

When something is lost in the park, to whom do we look but this ever-prepared beast which seems to secretly carry all things?

And when children think about the objects they have lost—dolls, teddy bears, flying rats, trees with seven voices (they can be hidden in only one place)—they remember the alpaca, their infinitely prepared companion.

But look at those eyes, those astonished eyes without knowledge; they only ask why she has been harnessed for such a long trip and why no one comes to relieve her.

The high plateau is to blame for this tragedy—the mother alpaca incessantly stares at it. The mountain was also casting off burdens, and so its summit became clear, and filled the eyes of the mother alpaca.

She was taken down from the plateau and situated near a nonsensical horizon, and when she turns her neck, she continues looking for the older alpaca, for the one who sheds a pack on high, and returns to the sun's radiance.

   "What have you and I done to our Andean cordillera?" I ask the alpaca.

THE COCONUT PALMS

We immediately recognize the coconut palms; they cannot be counted. For each dead Indian, the Spaniard planted a live palm, remaking the landscape, just as the race was remade in order to forget the former island, the home of Indians.

For forty days of my life, my eyes absorbed this new sky striped with vegetable necks, grooved with a million palm trees. A type of loom makes the warp, and allows the songs of birds and crazy insects to place the invisible weft, so rich with life.

After this, other skies will seem naked, devoid of the sovereign botanical core. The coconut palms are in a procession from Panateneas, a nomadic mass of coconut palms has created high ground with an unknown, orderly plan: palms united in a familiar party, exchanging friendly gestures. They touch heads and draw back their bodies. They dream with a tall hardness, but a melody always results below because of the long-haired heads bumping into each other, above.

IN PRAISE OF SALT

The great mounds of salt on the beach of Eve, dating from the year 3000, form a square forehead and square shoulders. Without a lukewarm dove or rose in hand, the rock gleams more than the seal on top of it. It has the power to transform everything into jewels.

The salt which whitens the gull's belly and rustles the penguin's breast plays on mother-of-pearl with colors that it doesn't own.

Salt is pure and absolute like death.

The salt which drives its spikes into the hearts of good people, even the heart of Jesus Christ, assures that they do not dissolve in piousness.

FLOUR

Flour is luminous and soft, the mother of abundance. Clear rice flour rustles like fine silk; starch is as fresh as the snowy water that relieves burns. From the humble potato, flour slips like silver. Such tender flours!

The heavy flour manufactured by the grief-filled spikes of rice or rye is as heavy as the Earth, the Earth herself that can create milky roads for creatures lacking original sin.

Smooth flour slides more silently than water and can fall over a naked child without waking him up.

Flour is clear and soft, the mother of abundance.

Maternal flour is the true sister of milk, almost a woman, a middle-class mother with a white hairdo and great breasts, sitting on a sunny threshold. She creates the flesh of children. She is supremely female, as womanly as rubber and chalk; she understands a lullaby if you sing it to her—she understands all womanly things.

If left alone in the world, she will nourish the planet with her round breasts.

She can also change herself into a mountain of milk, a smooth mountain where children roll incessantly.

Mother-flour is also an eternal daughter, rocked in the great folds of rice paddies, a little girl with whom the many winds invisibly play, caressing her face without getting to know it.

Clear flour. One can dust it over the poor, ancient black Earth, and she will return huge fields of daisies or decorations like frost.

Flour is clear and soft, the mother of abundance.

If she walked, no one would hear her cottony feet sink heavily into the land. If she wanted to dance, her serious arms would fall. If she sang, the song would get stuck in her thick throat. But she does not walk or dance or sing. If she wants to take a name, we must create a name for her with three Bs or three silken Ms.

THE LITTLE NEW MOON

It is in the sky—the new moon is looking at me–light as air. Twilight's enchantment still endures. In the hills, glorious afternoon tapestries linger, but amid this dazzling twilight, the new moon is a drop of sweetness; I set my eyes on it and smile. So, Francis, in the Father's sky, there are magnificent saints like Paul, rich with passion, and those like Augustine, rich as twilight gold, and others who form the great and violent West.

But my eyes have rested and want to reamain on you, a little new moon, thin as a golden hair, lost in the red sky.

BREAD

Vice of habit. Childhood's wonder, the magical feeling of materials and elements: flour, salt, oil, water, fire. Moments of pure vision, pure hearing, pure touch.

Life's consciousness in a moment. All memories swirl around bread.

It carries with it a very potent sensation of life, though I don't know by what interior approximation, an equally powerful thought of death. The thought of life becomes banal from the moment it does not mix with the thought of death. The pure essentials are superficial grandees or little pagans. The pagan takes care of both things.

THE FIG

Touch me: it is the softness of good satin, and when you open me, what an unexpected rose! Do you not remember some king's black cloak under which a redness burned?

I bloom inside myself to enjoy myself with an inward gaze, scarcely for a week.

Afterward, the satin generously opens in a great fold of long Congolese laughter.

Poets have not known the color of night, nor the Palestinian fig. We are both the most ancient blue, a passionate blue, which richly concentrates itself because of its ardor.

If I spill my pressed flowers into your hand, I create a dwarf meadow for your pleasure; I shower you with the meadow's bouquet until covering your feet. No. I keep the flowers tied—they make me itch; the resting rose also knows this sensation.

I am also the pulp of the rose-of-Sharon, bruised.

Allow my praise to be made: the Greeks were nourished by me, and they have praised me less than Juno, who gave them nothing.

Other Prose

CHILE

It is a territory so small that on the map it ends up seeming like a beach between cordillera and sea, a parenthesis of space whimsically situated between two centaur-like powers. To the south, the tragic caprice of southern archipelagos, shattered and in shards, creates great gashes in the velvet sea.

The zones are natural, clear, and definite, just like the character of the people. Northward, in the direction of the desert, the home of saltpeter, inflamed a second time by the sun, man's pain and strength are tested. Immediately, the zone changes to a place of mining and agriculture; it has instilled in us the most vigorous characteristics of our race: an austere, pastoral society, similar to the passionate asceticism of the Earth. Next, there is the agricultural zone, the affable countryside: festive fields of fruit trees, dense fields filled with regional workers where the peaceful shadow of the farmer passes by and breaks apart in transit through the valleys. At the same time, masses of agile workers labor like ants in the cities. In the extreme cold tropics, there exist forests which exhale breath like Brazilian air—but this tropical zone is black, deprived of the luxury of color. And there are islands with rich fishing waters, wrapped in violet mist, and finally the Patagonian tablelands, our unique land of wide skies, desolate, horizontal perfection, and snow-blanketed pastures for innumerable herds of cattle. It is a small territory, but not a small nation. The land is reduced, inferior to the spirit of its people. But that does not matter: we have the sea ... the sea ... the sea!

We are a new people and have not experienced Golden

Luck as a fairy godmother. Ours is the hard, Spartan mother of necessity. During the Indian period, the kingdom's influence was not extensive: wild tribes wandered through the sierras, seemingly blind to their destinies, which would provide the cement for the stupendous vigor of our race. Immediately, the Conquest began, cruel as everywhere else; the harquebus fired, until falling, empty, over the Araucanian's crocodilian back. Later, the Colony did not develop, as in the rest of America, clemency and refinement, a result of the silence of the defeated Indian; rather it was illuminated by the kind of awesome blinking lightning that the Mexican night possesses. Because of their struggle against the Indians, the conquistadors could not put down their arms and paint a pavan over their salons . . . Finally, the Republic came into being; slow and serene institutions were created . . . Some lackluster presidents only forewarned the necessity of heroic and passionate presidencies. Occasionally, some excelled, the zealous innovators: O'Higgins, Portales, Bilbao and Balmaceda.

Chile has experienced the minimum number of revolutions possible in our turbulent America: two wars in which the people exhibited the qualities of David, the shepherd who became a warrior and saved his people.

Now, within the deep pocket of mountains that was believed to be isolated from universal life, the world's rocky time, nevertheless, reverberates. The nation guards ardent palpitations within its neck, and it is like a resting lion. Its journey through republican life will probably always have leonine characteristics: a certain well-known severity of force, which when it becomes known, will not be exaggerated.

The race exists in a state of potent differentiation, and originality is a form of nobility. The Indian will come to be regarded as somewhat more exotic because of his scarcity. *Mestizos* blanket the territory and do not exhibit the weakness some note in races which are not pure.

We do not hate or even feel jealous of Europeans: the

white race will always be the civilizer, the one that has made order out of energy and forged collective organisms. The German has constructed and continues to construct the southern cities, working elbow-to-elbow with the Chilean, with whom he continues to communicate his sure sense of organization. The Yugoslav and the Englishman are involved in similar efforts in Magallanes and Antofagasta. Praised be the national spirit that allows cooperation in our sacred task of forming the eternal vertebrae of a nation, without hate, but with a noble understanding of what Europe sends to us.

We are not a refined race: the old and the rich are. We embody something of a primitive Switzerland; our austerity presses down forcefully upon the people from the hard mountains, but our ears ring, and the Greek invitation to the sea begins to kindle our spirits.

Poverty should sober us, without ever suggesting to us that we surrender to powerful countries that corrupt with insinuations of generosity. Sea-voyages opened Caupolicán's heart; this same need to travel is tattooed on our souls.

Mexico, August 1923

A PROFILE OF THE MEXICAN INDIAN WOMAN

The Mexican Indian woman possesses a very graceful profile. Often it is beautiful, but it is a very different kind of beauty than that to which our eyes have grown accustomed. Her skin, which lacks the rosiness of seashells, holds the brand of grain lavishly licked by the sun. Her eyes are the products of warm sweetness; her cheeks are finely drawn. Her forehead is moderate in size, as a feminine forehead should be. Her lips are neither inexpressively thin nor thick. Her accent is mellifluous, with a touch of sorrowful abandon—it is as though she always keeps a wide teardrop in the depths of her throat. The Indian woman is rarely fat. Slim and agile, she goes about her business with a bucket on her head or at her side, or with a baby, small as a bucket, on her shoulders. As in the case of her male companion, one sees in her body a refinement of essence in the small hill of her back.

The shawl gives her simple biblical lines. It is narrow and does not exaggerate her size with thick folds. It falls like tranquil water from the shoulders and knees. The ravelled-fringe edges give the effect of shimmering water. It is very beautiful. In order to show off its fineness, it is quite long and exquisitely variegated.

She almost always wears a blue shawl, marbled with white like jasper: it is like the prettiest painted egg I've ever seen! At other times, it is variegated with tiny strips of living color.

It surrounds her well; this encircling seems like the roundabout growth of the thick stem of the banana plant before a new, large leaf unfolds. Sometimes she wears the shawl on her head. It is not the many-cornered, coquettish mantilla which captures the image of a dark butterfly when worn over a woman's blonde hair. It is not a large, flowery cloak like a splendid carpet of tropical earth. The shawl soberly adorns her head.

With it, the Indian woman painlessly attaches her child to her shoulder. She is an old world woman, not free from her child. Her shawl surrounds him, just as he was surrounded inside of her womb by a thin and strong fabric made of her blood. On Sundays, she brings him to the market. While she haggles, the child plays with fruit or bright trinkets. With him at her side, she makes the longest journeys: she always wants to carry her joyous cargo. She still has not learned how to liberate herself...

Generally, her skirt is dark. But in some regions, for example, in the sultry zones, it does display the jubilant coloring of the gourd tree. The skirt spills when she raises it to walk, creating an eye-dazzling fan.

There are two feminine silhouettes that resemble flowers in form: the wide silhouette made by a large, pleated skirt and a puffy blouse, forming an open rose. The other is made with a straight skirt and simple blouse: it resembles the form of jasmine in which the long flower stalk dominates. The Indian woman is almost always endowed with this refined silhouette.

She walks incessantly, from the Puebla Sierra to the Uruapán farmlands, toward the cities. She marches on with naked feet, small feet that have not grown deformed despite the long distances traveled. (For the Aztec, big feet were the mark of a barbaric race.)

She walks on, swathed in the rain or in the sunshine, with luxuriant braids tied to the top of her head, dark in the solar glow. Sometimes she creates a glorious display of macaw plumage with multicolored yarn. She stops in the middle of a field, and I look at her. She is not shaped like the amphora: her hips are slender. She is a vase, a sun-gold vase from Guadalajara. Her cheeks are generously lapped by the oven's flame—by the

Mexican sun.

The Indian man tends to walk by her side. The shadow of his immense sombrero falls over the woman's shoulder; the whiteness of his suit is the countryside's lightning. They move quietly through pastoral gatherings. They pass from afternoon to afternoon with a word. From this I receive sweetness, without analyzing the feeling.

They had to have been a pleasure-loving race. God situated them like the first human couple, in a garden. But four hundred years of slavery have faded the equivalent glory of their sun and fruits. It has made their clay roads hard for them, when they are really soft, like spilled flesh.

And this woman who has not been praised by poets, with her Asiatic likeness, has to be kin to Ruth the Moabite: she toiled, and her face was blackened by a thousand siestas over heaps of unthreshed grain.

August, 1923

SOMETHING ABOUT THE QUECHUAN PEOPLE

In the skirted hills of the central Peruvian sierra, inside a stony amphitheater into which falls the purest Andean light, there once existed one of the most exotic peoples in the world, the Quechuan race, the matrix of the Incan empire.

In spite of the evident diligence of the historians, little is known about their origin, and even less is known when it comes to understanding how they were able to organize, in less than a thousand years, that which sociologists call "the miracle of the Incanato."

Reading the Inca Garcilaso, Prescott or Boudin, one never knows if one is reading a divine story from the Golden Age or a real document of Indo-American experience. This culture was wise and new, and at the same time, primitive and technical, imperial and peace loving. It drew the strength of its regime and the poetry of its inner life from two springs which were almost alike: a religion based on astronomy and a sense of aristocracy, that is to say, a political structure applied to the common good for collective profit. They adored the sky and had a long line of astral, atmospheric divinities, while in the meantime, neighboring tribes were eating human flesh and had bestial or grotesque gods. The Incan People, or that is, their governing religious aristocracy, believed themselves to be direct children of the sun, and their Pantheon, from the star-father to the rainbow and lightning entities, knew everything about heavenly or telluric matters.

Despite a certain infantilism, the faith of the Quechuan

religion evolved beyond the Asian religions, with the exception of Hinduism. It surpassed Buddhism.

The empire extended from Columbia to Chile and from the Pacific to the Eastern coast of Bolivia and the head of Argentina. This superabundance of land was obtained through a minimum of warfare. The Inca conquered nearby Indian tribes with accomplished skill and more than patriarchal benevolence; the art and mysticism of the conquest consisted of solemn and friendly excursions made by the Inca and their court to neighboring lands, retinues with the mission of revealing the magnificence and gentility of the Empire, thus catechizing the uncivilized neighbors who always ended up loyal to the Incanato.

It was commonplace for the savages to be convinced and conquered by this crusade, which was more verbal than military, more political than aggressive.

The Quechua knew and practiced the majority of today's occupations; their farmers produced exactly what was needed to sustain the people. The area of arable land was roughly twice that which the subsequent Spanish regime incorporated. The Asiatic Quechua, who suffered so much and were amazing in their exactitude, invented farming on terraces and terrepleins in order to conquer and empower the sour Andean land of rocks and poor earth, which they chose for themselves instead of the lush, tropical lands. For the love of thin air and proximity to the sky, and in order to live as close as possible to the heavens he adored, the Quechua rejected the warm and sensual lower zones.

An Indian, with a body sharp as arrows, austere as his cactuses, and stubborn as volcanic rock, converted the cordilleras into great steppes of corn, a plantation of potatoes, an emporium of vegetables and fruit trees. This falsely-labeled "primitive"considered abandoning the earth a crime against the sun, against the Inca, and his children. In order to cultivate, through pure will, the bitter Andes, a task which seemed absurd, the Quechua had to plan, construct and maintain a system of artificial irrigation. At an altitude of 3,488 meters, there was no river at their disposal. But there were waterways of all kinds: trenches, stone canals, torrent correctors; the Quechua forsaw, envisioned and implemented them.

Their excursions were not enough to obtain supplies; starting with cotton, a hundred products from the lowlands had to be brought up to the cold sierra. And so, the narrow Andean empire was enlarged, encompassing wide plains and semi-tropical valleys.

From the cliff at Cuzco, the Inca could witness the Andean vastness they governed, and with his imperial vision, he planned conquests and the unification of the regions acquired. The empire, which was called Tihuantinsuyo, that is, "the four parts of the world," demanded unification, and this brought about the need for roads.

The Incanato constructed a network of roadways, starting from the sacred heart of Cuzco. This involved chewing up, hacking apart and conquering nothing less than the Andean cordillera.

From stone, another empire arose; Incan roadways and paths shaped like the boa and small snake, came and went, joining the provinces with huge, white stitches, narrowing the secret pockets of the cordillera, clearing chasms by the use of rope bridges, and so linking the Quito, the Chilchas, the Changos, etc. . . . with the vital heart of the sacred capital, seat of the major solar temples and residence of the sun-loving Inca. In this way, they constructed, Roman style, the organism and circulatory system of an Indian empire that seems fabulous— but it was real. For the Incanato, it was important that after a conquest, it stood guard to supplant the savage customs of adjacent tribes and cultivate its own, to expel the puerile, lowly demi-gods and sow its own religion with all the force of the wind. The roads served these goals like human beings; they were worth more than armies.

The Inca would achieve much more because of their genius for organization. The Incan clan, which was patriarchal in civil matters and matriarchal in religious matters, attempted to create a Utopia, the abolition of absolute misery, that poverty which at its lowest point creates subhuman conditions. The Inca experimented and achieved as much as a daring plan could render. It came very close to success, and almost hit the impossible mark. Idleness was unknown in Tihuantinsuyo; every man had at least one job, and sometimes two. Thanks to universal employment, a specialized work force of men and women (the elderly were exempt), a straw roof protected each family from the Andean ice; good cotton clothing always warmed the body of the Andean man, and no child of the sun lacked precious and exact rations of corn, potatoes, and fruit in prosperous years or in the times of meager harvests. But naturally, there was nothing soft or idyllic about this state, which excelled in authoritarianism and which was doubly austere in matters of imperialism and theology. Housing, feeding and clothing one fourth of the continent, an entire flank of the Americas, could never be an enterprise of butter or sugarcane.

Because of this, Tihuantisuyo was a place of harsh customs and harsh discipline–it seemed basaltic.

Along the Andes, one could see the sacred spectacle of men kneeling over their springs boring holes in stone without knowledge of the gimlet, or in other ways disturbing the poor earth without the aid of a wheeled plough.

Despite this, the Spartan empire was tempered and humanized by two things: a pagan astronomical cult devoid of human sacrifices or other cruelties, and the long festival of successful work in four or six majestic crafts.

The Quechua had a popular and religious epic theater; they created a spinnery for colored cloths, and even those of ancient Egypt could not rival their product. They were like a Chinese version of the American, equipped with sophisticated eyes and hands. The Quechua developed a method of making ceramics comparable to Etruscan and Assyrian efforts, and finally, their pagan mystical cult trained them in ritual dance and song. Of both, little more than fragments, pieces for dance or drum or quena-flute music, survive. I have received these melancholic remains; they hold the bruised markings of a race that was to be defeated in body and soul.

The complex and wise Incanato, in addition to all that has been told, had a curious and valuable body of functionaries, unknown even to classical civilizations: they were the Amautas. Their mission was quite diversified. The Amauta chronicled city life, therefore playing the role of historian; he preached imperial and religious patriotism which conformed with Indian theocracy, and the Amauta recited and sometimes produced poetry.

What a beautiful vocation for a man! The Amauta served as a medium for inspiration but also organized solemn and popular festivals. Today we would say that he provided the people with the bread of happiness. The business of the Amauta was laden with honor but also with seduction. Perhaps his was the only profession I have envied or longed for in solitude, desiring it for myself or saddened because it no longer exists.

One can see then how the Incanato truly provided an entire network of necessities for its people; today we would employ that ugly word—the "masses." The grave and harsh regime had its charms, its pauses for refreshment, even its heights of joy.

July, 1947

THE CHILEAN *COPIHUE*

The climbing vine classified with the Gallic-Latin name *Lapagiere Rosea* is first a simple surprise and then a delight for the explorers and tourists who reach the forests of Southern Chile.

Geographers call this region "The Cold Tropics," and although the label might appear contradictory, it corresponds with those truths which wear an absurd face: the southern region of Chile is wet and frosty, but it resembles the tropics in its vigorous vegetation and exhalation of aromatic vapors. For this reason, no traveler reaches Chile and remains there without getting to know our southern forests, and no one leaves that region either without searching for, or bumping into, the Araucanian *copihue*.

Scholarly texts confound children with this fact: the completely indigenous copihue is related by name to . . . the Empress Josephine Bonaparte! I am just as scandalized by this fact as the children are, but wise ones do the christening; the Adam of science of the Creole people has not yet been born, and it was Frenchmen who christened our flower without taking into account its Indian complexion . . . Well, at least Josephine was a Creole Frenchwoman from Martinique. Let the Latin name remain in scholarly texts; within Chile it will only be called the *copihue*, which is better spelled with the *h* than with the *g* some use. (The aspirant *h*, well-loved by the Quechua-Aymara, is more airy-sounding than the heavy g; it seems like the breath of the very thing being named. It caresses and it does no harm.)

The *copihue* flower climbs in brusque staircases of color

from Buddhist white through carmine. The red flowers sound an alarm, the pink ones don't quite blush, and the white ones hang from branches like tiny baby hands. The first color is most popular and captivates with a triumph that seems electoral, but I prefer the loser, that is, the white *copihue* and its form, a pure vegetable star. The bullish preference for red is the same one that makes victorious, with one violent wink, the explosive carnation and the bloody rose.

The narrow, bell-shaped flower, actually more a tube than a bell, disturbs the sense of touch with an oily texture like the camelia's. The *copihue's* extensive breath is not exhaled into the upper atmosphere; it sinks into the Earth's greenness. Instead of swelling up straight with pride, it bends with a mystifying Indian languor because of its very slim stem. The *copihue's* languidness seems liquid; the vine lets its flowers fall in droplets or in tears.

More sought after than the *huemul,* the vine is no longer found in forests immediately near population centers or highways. The searcher has to employ guesswork to pursue it, but it will surely be easier to find than the obscure little Chilean deer.

Cast over the sides of laurel trees, sometimes gracefully flowing and covering it, it is very feminine, with a whim for hiding and reappearing suddenly. Whether in great dappled clusters, or hanging in festoons, or in rivulets of red-hot coals, the *copihue* sends sparkles over the shadowy greenness. For the searcher with his powder flashes, they swirl up into the canopies of trees, extending themselves like Indian guerillas.

The climbing vine shatters the angry austerity of the southern forest; it starves it and almost casts it out of all conversation. It is the acrobat of oak trees and a dancer in the white-woods; it vexes its teacher-trees with silken twists from flaming rockets. Less violent than the *guacamayas,* but forming similar bands, the hanging vines of the *copihue* stir up passions and shriek over the shoulders of the vegetable Methuselahs.

I am stirred by the popular metaphor that compares our

flower with the blood of speared Indians, but I don't want to repeat the tale or lie. The *copihue* does not remind me of blood, but of fire, cascading ribbons of liberated fire and homemade flame, fatuous and diurnal fire—it is the good and the bad, the fire of all myths.

The gadfly vine, stinging with the forest, sets traps like all igneous spirits: it is an elf in verdant escapades, a mischievous hobgoblin and also a hot-blooded fire sprite. What fearless, great saints the tall trees prove themselves to be, bitten here and there by the red pincers that bind and unbind them in abusive wiry tangles! At times, the larch or cinnamon tree look just like Gulliver, mocked by the climber moving nimbly through the entanglements.

What subtle and beautiful power you have, *Copihue*! Although you just barely hook the great giant with your ray, you win over all eyes and make them forget about the entire tree. Because you cause this division, the child or the woman no longer gazes at the teacher-tree, but at the intruder balancing itself near heaven: half lamp, half jewel. An explanation for their superabundance: only in the case of the orchid did God, the sculptor, create more and better flowers than the *copihues*. (And these two parasites that run their marathon as champions among flowers have in common elegant grace and the misfortune of not having any fragrance).

The *copihue*, a marvelous prodigy, had to inspire myths. It is certain that it traveled from the Bio-Bio to the Bueno in love songs, and during time of war, it vanished. When the Indian loses his land, what remains inevitably vanishes with him, or for a time, crawls over the dust before expiring.

Poets constantly celebrate the botanical emblem of our nation. The Penquista tends to say: "Verdugo Cavada spoke to the *copihue* and Perez Freire made it sing." So it is: the best of our popular musicians adopted the already well-known red flower; it ventures through the air in songs passing from mouth to mouth, from Patagonia to the Aleutian Islands.

After these songs of fortune, honors have been showered upon the southern vine; teachers speak effervescently about its botanical qualities, elaborating with repeated pleasure and love. They exalt the local flower as part of a kind of patriotic cate-chism. The pencils of children rejoice in creating its form, and the *copihue* competes in sketchbooks with the nation's flag, repeating one of its colors, almost in competition with its star.

Soon it will reach stadiums and university auditoriums to crown the champions and those who wear togas during solemnities. The tables of Luculo, made to order at official ban-quets, already have adopted it as the flower to adorn its footpaths or stone walkways, or as a decoration for tablecloths. (Although the *copihue* proves useless for creating a fragrant vase or bou-quet, it does make a very good garland; also, it is a naturally excellent garland, unlike the thorny rose or hard-arched jas-mine).

Like good love, this passion has a solid foundation. The *copihue* was well-suited to be born and situate itself in Chile's extremities where the globe of the Earth plunges into one last sharp curve and is covered with chills. But before coming to an end, the Earth's work became angelic with the creation of ferns, mosses and the *copihues,* which frighten the nearby snow with their fire. (Thus, Magellan would have been terrified by the bon-fires of the last strait).

I have tried to spread the news about my Indian *copihue,* and by telling about it, give it to the reader. But as I complete this, I realize the futility of the endeavor. Nothing is rendered real in words, not the flower, not the exotic fruit. When a Mexican who was visiting Chile told me about his golden mango, I was not able to savor the shape or juice of the beautiful fruit: learning is receiving. When in Puerto Rico, I listened to the rose-apple being praised, but the fragrant morsel did not enter my mouth or cross my teeth. It is God's will that each fruit and flower be direct initiations. To "know them" means to inhale their aromas and to taste them, and since for me, the newness of each species of fruit and flower is worth as much as a new country, and nothing less, I say to you, the reader, that if you want to possess the Chilean *copihue,* go to Cautin to see it; don't buy it in the train stations, but venture into the forest and break off a piece of it with an eager tug . . . Don't believe that you have learned something because you have read a few zealously written and worthless pages from a storyteller who has delivered this vignette, in vain . . .

Petropolis, Brazil, July 1943

Huemul — a species of Chilean deer. There is debate as to whether the huemel has become extinct or still exists.

Guacamayas—Chilean Indians.

Bio-Bio and the Bueno—Chile's two major rivers.

Penquista – An inhabitant of the city of Concepcion.

ALFONSINA STORNI

I have been told: "Alfonsina is ugly," and so I expect to see a face less pleasing than the voice I listen to on the telephone, a face something like the punishment given to a creature who conceals her inner excellence. So, when I open the door and meet Alfonsina, I stand there for a moment, amazed, and I even have the bold candor to ask, "Alfonsina?—" "Yes, Alfonsina," she laughs, a good, cordial laugh.

Her hair is extraordinary, but not because of any unsightly characteristics. It is completely silver, and that distinguishes the face of this twenty-five year old. I have never seen a lovelier head of hair: it is wonderfully unusual, midday moonlight. It was once golden, and some sweet blond memory still lingers in the white clusters.

Faithful eyes, an exalted and elegant French nose, and her skin of roses give Alfonsina a somewhat childlike appearance, concealing the sagacious speech of a mature woman. She is small, very lithe, and the overall manner of her gestures is jaspered (the expression fits) with intelligence.

This is our Alfonsina. Very little of her physical being is our creation, that is, very little is "American." I have a strong curiosity about bloodlines and begin to take notes . . . Alfonsina surprises me with the fact that she was born in Switzerland, in Italian Switzerland. Directly after that declaration, she tells me about her voluntary adoption of Argentina and her education. It is, more exactly, her adoption of Buenos Aires; she does not possess any characteristic of the Argentine Creole. Alfonsina is a new American, a product of European blood galvanized under our sun. Her eyes are generously made in order to examine the generosities of the pampa; she is the future American, a gracefully agile tennis player who doesn't display the physical bulk of the rather plump Creole. She is a human of splendid individuality: her mother gazed at the Mediterranean and received the Atlantic's face in reply.

I will spend seven days with her, and I must confess that I somewhat dread the meeting, without ceasing to desire it—I am eager to experience the best of this world. Letters brought us a little closer together. Alfonsina, unlike an American, tends to write epistles, perversely desiring to lead her correspondents off the right track. Perhaps this defense against calamity has become the norm for correspondence among people of literature. The Alfonsina of my letters was egotistical, a joker, and sometimes, voluntarily banal. A good amount of unspoken trepidation forms my fear of the meeting: I have unilateral interests, and am far from being a rich creature, who like the bountiful Earth, harbors creations of endless originality and an ability to please the masses. Naturally, like the roadside innkeeper, I fear that my guest might not like my corn and ordinary milk.

This anguish enjoys a short life. I do not talk about matters of little interest to Alfonsina, and she does not mention things which alienate me. I have encountered few women so skilled in human behaviour: I don't tire of her ways. She doesn't make me feel eager to conceal myself from her. She is more expansive than Juana, who was a good descendent of Basques and built fortresses for herself. The feast of her friendship is created through intelligence; she demonstrates little emotion. This turns out to be an advantage; the effusion of the American earth I tread can become tiresome, like an extravagant countryside. She is profound, when she wants to be, without fading into oblivion—she is profound because she has suffered the deep wound of life. And she is happy, but not happy like the parti-colored tapestries of people given to excess. Hers is an elegant joy, transformed into a game. She pays much attention to whomever is at her side; it is the attention of pure intelligence, but it is a kind of love. Like few of life's creatures, she enjoys a wealth of knowledge, and offers opportune commentaries about the most diverse matters. She is a metropolitan women who passes through life, touching everything, and incorporating herself. Alfonsina is one of those people who can experience understanding with the mind as well as the emotions, a very Latin thing.

She exhibits simplicity, and I must repeat, an elegant simplicity. Today many crass people are parading by us, and they sicken us, as much as preciousness, Alfonsina's enemy. She doesn't exhibit ingenuousness or pedantry, but rather a sense of inner security which never becomes boastful. It is the security of someone who has measured her strength during a life of hardships and is content with herself. With a grin, she tells me, accentuating a trait that is characteristically her own, "Alfonsina wants to be ready for everything."

Words do not do justice to this poet. Perhaps she is the Argentine poet to be ranked after Lugones. Faraway critics, those who do not write commentaries in order to inflict pain upon another or to receive in return some advantage, have showered her with great praise. She is on Juana's side, the one we admire, by virtue of her rich poetry, encompassing all motives. Poetry is varied by her humanity: a merciful, cruel, bitter and playful humanity. The extensive praise exceeds her expectations.

With Alfonsina, I experience heightened moments, our thoughts become one, as when she shares the total appreciation that we owe to Delmira Agustini: "She is the best of us and we should not forget it," Alfonsina tells me. It makes me happy to hear this: it is an obsolete practice in America to attribute exact worth to the living, while continuing to admire the dead.

"Yes, Alfonsina," I answer her. "She was and continues to be the best, irrevocably the best. If we forget her, it is because our race still does not understand that which could be called the guardianship of the old dead: how to honor them in an ordinary way, and love them so that they might pardon the imperfect hand we use to glorify them."

The nearness of Alfonsina fills me with the great pleasure of finding among our new people a completely developed soul, worthy of an ancient race. But there is one thing more: she is a woman who has battled life's ugliness; she retains the friendly soul awarded to those who are helped, or those who simply help themselves.

Paris, March, 1926

GABRIELA THINKS ABOUT HER ABSENT MOTHER

Mother, within the depths of your womb, my eyes, my mouth, and my hands were made in silence. With your richest blood, you irrigated my body, just as water irrigates the bulbs of hyacinths, hidden underground. My senses are yours, and with this as the gift of your flesh, I make my way through the world. I praise you for all the earthly splendor that enters me and casts a net around my heart.

Mother, I grew like a fruit on a thick branch, upon your knees. They still hold my body's imprint—another child hasn't erased them. You got so used to rocking me. When I ran through the streets, you remained in the hallway of our home, apparently sad because you would no longer feel my weight.

There is no rhythm among the hundred rhythms overflowing from the first music more tender than your rocking, Mother. The peaceful things existing in my soul came together with the swaying of your arms and knees.

With the two, you rocked me and continued singing to me; the verses were nothing more than playful words, pretexts for your own.

You used their songs to name earthly things: hills, fruit trees, people, denizens of the countryside. It was as though you were trying to make your daughter feel at home by pointing out each family member in this world where you placed her to live. How strange.

And so, I continued to get to know your hard and soft universe: there is not one small word used to name the creatures of this world that I did not learn from you. Only later did teachers repeat the sweet sounding names you offered me.

Mother, you continued to lead me near innocent things I could touch without hurting myself: an herb from the vegetable patch, a tiny, color-splashed stone. When I touched these things, I experienced the fellowship of all creation. Sometimes you bought or made toys for me: a doll with huge eyes like mine, a little playhouse purchased on sale . . . But I didn't love those dead toys. You remember: my best toy was your body.

I played with the hairs on your head as though they were little threads of slippery water. I played with your round chin and with your fingers which I intricately crossed and uncrossed. For your daughter, the face you lowered was the most wonderful sight on earth. I gazed curiously at your fluttering eyelids and the play of light within your green eyes—and that very strange look of yours when you became upset, Mother!

Yes, my entire small world was your face, your cheeks like hillocks of honey, and the furrows engraved by suffering near the edges of your mouth: two small, tender valleys. I learned about forms by observing your face: your eyelashes quivering like little blades of grass and the plant stems in your neck. When your turned toward me, you creased the air with friendship. And when I learned to walk hand-in-hand with you, attached like a live pleat to your skirt, I ventured away to learn, to get to know our valley.

Fathers are too full of troubles to take us by the hand and walk or climb hills with us.

We are more your children. We grow surrounded by you, in the same way the almond is surrounded and enclosed in its shell. The sky we most love is not the one full of cold and limpid stars—it is the other, with your eyes so near, close enough to kiss tears away.

The father trudges through life's heroic bedlam, and we know nothing of his day. We only observe that during the afternoon he returns and usually deposits a small pile of fruit on the table. We see him give the linen and flannel for the family wardrobe, and you use this material to clothe us. But the one who peels the fruit for the child's mouth, and the one who juices the fruit during the sweltering siesta, is you, Mother. The one who cuts the flannel and linen into small pieces and turns them into a suit of love which clings fast to the child's chilly ribs, is you, poor Mother, oh most tender one!

The child already knows how to walk and how to piece together small words like colored glass. Then you place a light prayer at the center of his tongue, and it remains there until his last day. This prayer is as plain as a lily's stem—so love and clear vision upon the Earth: we ask for our daily bread and affirm that men are our brothers. We praise the vigorous will of God.

In this way, the one who shows us the Earth as an extended canvas of lavish forms and colors also helps us to understand our hidden God.

I was a sad child, Mother, a shy little girl like the dark crickets in daylight; like the green lizard, I drank up the sun. It hurt you to see that your little girl did not play like the other children. You would say that I had a fever, when in the vineyard outside of our house, you discovered me talking to the gnarled vines and the slim, graceful almond tree—to me it seemed like an enchanted little boy!

Now once again I am talking to you that way, but you aren't able to answer me. If you could see me, you would put your hand on my forehead and repeat as in the past: "Daughter, you have a fever."

Mother, all those who have come after you preach their lessons over what you have already taught me. They use many words to say things you said with few. Our ears grow weary, and the pleasure of listening to a story wanes. Your little girl learned things more pleasantly: the lessons were so well learned over your heart. You placed your knowledge upon me like a golden wax of love; you didn't speak out of obligation, and so, you didn't rush. You poured your soul into your little girl. You never demanded that I remain quiet and stiff, listening to you, on a hard bench. While I listened to you, I played with the back of your blouse or the pearl shell buttons of your sleeve. And Mother, this is the only joyful education I've ever known.

Then I became a teenager, and then a woman. I have walked alone, without your body's protection, and I know that this thing called freedom is something devoid of beauty. I have witnessed my shadow fall, ugly and depressed, over the countryside, without yours, so small, by my side. I have also spoken, without necessity, of your support. I desired that, like before, your words of guidance might be found in every one of my sentences. I wanted the extension of my voice to become a garland of our two voices.

Now I speak to you with my eyes closed, forgetting where I find myself. My eyes are tightly sealed; I don't see the very wide sea between your heart and my face. I speak to you as if I were touching your clothing. My hands are half-open, and I imagine I am clutching your hand.

I've already told you—I wear flesh borrowed from you; I speak with the lips you made for me; with your eyes, I examine foreign lands. You also see tropical fruits through these eyes— the heavy pineapple exhales its perfume; the orange overflows with light. With my pupils, you enjoy the contours of these other mountains, so different from the fleeceless mountain under which you raised me! Through my ears, you hear the talk of people who possess an accent sweeter than ours. And you understand and cherish them. At a certain moment, you are torn to pieces inside of me; homesickness becomes like a burn; my eyes remain wide open, but I don't see the Mexican landscape.

I give thanks today, and every day, for the capacity you gave me to gather the Earth's beauty: it is like the water gathered by one's lips. I also thank you for the painful riches I carry within the depths of my heart, without knowing death.

In order to believe that you hear me, I have lowered my eyelids and hurl this morning away from me, believing the after-

noon now covers you. To tell you the rest, words break apart. I
am going to remain silent.

1923

THE TROPICAL DESTINY OF SOUTH AMERICA

Like Africa and Australia, our southern continent is a massive formation. It is truly what geographers call a closed continental mass, meaning that it tenuously extends the stalks of peninsulas into the sea. The continent has scarcely been eroded or diminished by the ocean, as in the case of Europe. Only Africa presents a more powerful inner nucleus, and, after it, Asia; but Asia lets fall festoons of southern peninsulas, and thus neutralizes the disadvantages of overpowering continentalism.

The antimaritime character of our geography does not stop the seafaring world from seeking and serving us, but it has restructured coastal trading quite a bit.

There existed two great and valid remnants of the coast: the magnificent Golfo de Plata and the graceful pocket-like formation of Maracaibo; at the center lies the Amazon Delta with its anthill islands, which lack the exact perfection of the first example. The awesome southern bays of Argentina are still truly unexploited lands, and therefore, have no prosperous ports. One can say the same thing about Chile's dissected southern coast.

In few places is the powerful attraction of the sea as visible as in South America. The girdled coast suits the concentration of its inhabitants. Capital cities are located in the interior, but always relatively near the sea. It is enough to note this detail to understand that we are part of a land shaped by those who came from the sea, and, naturally, they founded their capitals close to the roads of arrival, and retreat, in case of bad luck.

The vast, empty interior of the continent may be attributed not only to matters of climate; it is believed that the aboriginal race proved weak when faced with such a titanic environment. The people did not have the skill or desire to confront the continent's heart. They searched for, and found, merciful land upon the plateaus, although it proved sterile; in the meantime, they neglected the enormous natural bounty of the entire Amazon. The interior of Africa, with a similar climate, has always retained and nourished more people than the Amazon flatlands.

The tropical destiny of South America becomes very visible, by degrees, from Cabo San Rogue to the Tumbes Peninsula, corresponding with the continent's greatest width.

As we approach the temperate southern zones, our land becomes explicitly slender; it forms no part of the northern temperate zone. That which we now consider the temperate zone of the south is made worldly; it is the definitive geography: the tropics strengthen us; we are, for the sake of excellence, a fiery land. Greater tropical domination is seen only in Africa. For many centuries we will continue gnawing, taking advantage only of the continent's maritime garland, living in poverty at the door of the Amazon's blazing hearth.

June, 1930

AN AMERICAN MYTH: CHILE'S *EL CALEUCHE*

In Southern Chile, where the map depicts Chiloe and its retinue of islands as round dots, and further south, where almost everything is water, land becomes scarce until the solid land of Patagonia juts forward. Not far away flow two great rivers, the Bueno and the Maullin, and the sea behaves capriciously, chipping away at the cordilleras, creating worthless archipelagos, chopping up peninsulas and fjords. Water spirits are more powerful than earthly ones, keeping the Chilote and Patagonian on alert.

The sun shows itself four months out of the year over these places where the fog holds more phantoms than in any other region of South America, a continent of fruit and sunshine. Hazy monsters wallow in this sea, elsewhere clear and without complexities.

When the night completely seals itself off and becomes like a coffer, becoming so very long that it seems never to want to end, the old ones and the Chilor children, or both, in turn, recount all that is known, as only the old and children can: the true story of the "Caleuche, a Ship of Art."

The Caleuche is a pirate ship, a wicked manifestation of the noble sea. To better fulfill its adventures, it journeys underwater for miles and miles, adroitly concealed. For weeks and months, all traces of it vanish, and it seems as though it has at last died or abandoned the sea of the Chilotes. The sea made a pact with the ship it seems, and from the beginning of time, the sea has kept its promise to hide the ship, along with its white coral and the fish of nightmares. All of a sudden, on one very lonely southern night, the Caleuche surfaces like a shot with its whale of a body, and it travels a good distance, visible to the eye, navigating with all its machinery (if it has any), almost flying. Neither a whaling ship nor a fishing boat could catch up to it, if the idea occurred to them.

In the eyes of fisherman, crazy with fear, it manifests itself as a huge phosphorescent body, from bow to stern. It doesn't have sails—they would be useless! A secret deck seethes with sea devils and a tribe of warlocks settled among them. The complete effect of its cargo and the accoutrements of passage create the atmosphere of an offshore festival of Kermes. The Caleuche races through the sea to a very great, solemn appointment.

A "motor" propels the ship with dolphin speed. One does not know where it begins or ends. It seems to be powered by petroleum or alcohol and to have departed from an undersea forge of sea metals. It is driven by "Art," implemented by the high command of practitioneers of oceanic witchcraft.

Hunters of the illuminated prey draw near, but before they can get a good look and capture its secret, the Caleuche's palace comes to a dead stop. Its lights are extinguished, and the ship looks like a great piece of half-charred wood. A large, lifeless tree trunk remains: dark embers floating, drifting among the waves, deceiving those who painted victory banners.

One cannot speak of the Caleuche with exactitude because it does not resemble any other thing but . . . the Caleuche. We are put in a bind to define it, and we fumble the negotiations. It is not a whale, although it resembles one in terms of its skill for capsizing fishing boats. It is not a true ship, although it is proclaimed one, if only because it validly navigates eternal waters.

The Caleuche carries with it, well, a crew that we'll refer to as luminous devils and warlocks "of great art." We know nothing about these angels, except their anti-angelic indolence. As for the warlocks, we know that their faces are twisted and backwards, and their left legs are gnarled like their faces, and in addition, they are dwarfed. They prowl the deck, hopping on one foot, creatures absurd for life.

From time to time, the Caleuche takes men from the coast; perhaps they are captured, or someone goes crazy and jumps on deck. They, and the others, are lost souls: when their journey ends, and they again touch earth, they return with back-ward-twisted bodies, like those who remained on the ship, but, in addition, they forfeit all their memories. They will never recall what they witnessed on the illuminated ship, because the guardians of "the Art" do not want someone with a loose tongue to reveal what he has seen and learned. And so, the idiots lose the best thing that they received from the God who created them: they leave their memories in a house of wonders.

The monstrous ship is known for only one good deed. When it seized its Christian crew's love, and knowing their child-of-Adam's appetite for money, it handed over to them fireships laden with gold which they had desired to take hold of in the bay. And it did more, consenting to approach land. Face to face with the houses of Chilote, the ship allowed the crew to carry their wineskins to a friendly door. The family of the Caleuche's servant quickly became rich—and without a visible cause. The master of the house always avoided speaking to those who questioned him about his overnight wealth; he would do nothing but smile in the crafty manner of a Chilote, without allowing a confession to slip . . . and so, he managed his escape.

The Caleuche is eternal, and its navigators never age. Its withered old men weave tales of the Earth's witchcraft, but the sea creatures picture themselves as forever juvenile. The "mute" or the "transformed" ones that the Caleuche carries breathe pure sea breezes; they sleep during the day and celebrate at night, and since this navy is descended from Ulysses, neither the demon-masters, nor the warlock-slaves grow tired of their debauchery.

The sailors of the Caleuche do not marry when they reach the coasts, where girls who want to find a mate play on the dunes or gather clams. Not in Llicaldad, Trini-Tren or Quicari, their potential homelands, have the great beast or its baptized warlocks carried away young beauties. They remain bachelors, like Doctor Faustus. And because they do not have wives or children, the Caleuche seems like the Wandering Jew who only wears the air over his ribs and the Earth that he takes and leaves behind.

Travelling across the southern sea, we all encounter the Caleuche, without seeing it. Each southern tide has tasted and touched the Caleuche. The Patagonian Pulche feels it the moment it takes its chest out of the water.

The Caleuche wanders and returns again. We do not know where it lawlessly navigates or what mission is fulfilled when its journey ends. It returns with unique arrogance. And if it travels simply for the sake of travelling, it must happen because, like seamen, it came to adore the salt and now cannot exist on the Earth where we drink sweet water.

Nocturnal fishermen of inner seas glimpse a flank of the ship, but those who sleep soundly miss the vision. Lighthouse guardians, with their eyes pressed to the sea, have seen it once or many times. Perhaps they are simply fools—or eyewitnesses to a miracle. Those who stay up all night on promontories or crags receive pleasure mixed with fright. When they behold the otherworldly Caleuche, the pleasure translates more easily into storytelling than feeling. The true Chilote, a cowboy of the archipelago, weatherbeaten and briny, always wins a chance to behold the vision and carries with him for the rest of his life eyes illuminated by the ship's brilliance. This enchanted Chilote will compose the romance or tale of the Caleuche:

It shines upon the sea like something from another life.

It is a shame that those who really know the Caleuche, apart from the idiots it heaves up on the shores, do not tell us more. They are the sea-folk the pirates drowned when they capsized their ships. These creatures dwell at the bottom of the sea, their fairytale tongues eaten away by octopi, and their gesturing arms broken by the sponger fish of the deep, the swordfish.

Lisbon, June 193?

"Caleuche, a Ship of Art"— Magical art.

THE ARGENTINE PAMPA

At last, this is Argentina! After the solemn and fantastic Uspallata Valley with its lion-like mountains which for a long time extend my vision of Chile, the pampa comes.

For someone raised in the mountains, entangled in the mountain's voice, for someone used to leaping from mountain to mountain, the pampa cannot be beautiful. The eyes of a resident of the pampa must feel equally disoriented when they travel to the other side of the Andes. Our mountains are great; they exude an air of secret defense, a mysterious and vast presence of guidance and companionship. The worker who waters our cornfield, and the engineer who designs a road through the central plain, and the children who play under the willow tree, grandfather of the countryside, are all similarly guided by the mountains. In the pampa, eyes have no place to fix themselves; vision becomes distracted, vagabond and lax. After only a few moments, we are not looking at the real pampa, but rather a version the soul has conjured for us. Don't say that this spectacular sight is like the sea! The sea, a unity of lush life, does not allow a person to look at it with laxness. Someone once called it a peacock, and truly, it does show off with insistent vanity.

But this pampa, whose beauty is less perfect than that of the mountains or the sea, was made to sustain people. For a time they disdained it, and an Argentine tells me that Sarmiento used to speak with great pain about the horrendous distances this useless thing created. Today the Argentines would not trade it for the diamond mines of South Africa or one of those lands rich with mind-dazzling fountains of crude oil. Perhaps the

Argentine pampa forms a part of the Earth made with human necessities in mind. It seems that man's will, and not the insensate impetus of nature, labored to create these outskirts, places of exhaustion for the horse, guanaco and fallow buck. There exist regions equally vast—and even richer: the Amazon flatlands. But they do not possess the innocent promise of this place, its simple surrender. With its smoothness and grandeur, we can call it a world greener than the sea. A child who is born here, and who never abandons the place, could easily believe that the pampa encircles the planet like the atmosphere, and outside of it, nothing else exists.

Cornfields pass by; swamps surrounded by abandoned earth pass; high pastures pass; groups of trees and haciendas pass. The pampa has emptied Europe, and it could empty Asia.

If the physical characteristics of a country give it a moral tonic, Argentina has always been a generous land. Such was its geographic destiny, a kind of imperative of the plain. And among the missions of humanity—the heroic mission, the mission to dominate, the mission to civilize—the pampa's destiny involves welcoming the haphazard human overflow of other continents—and it is as noble as the desire to civilize. Receiving masses of human beings also means organizing them, and since these are masses of white people, it also means providing them with familiar surroundings.

As the train crosses the pampa, I remember *The Song of Argentina* by our Rubén Darío, a visionary of all American extremes. The song develops in keeping with the breadth and sovereign liberty of the pampa; it exudes the joy of this green river, and exhales from its depths, the secret gift of an eternal treasure. Above and beyond all, the song brings feeling to the presence of an advocation: such generosity, the greatest generosity! Darío knew, forty years ago, that Europe would move on to another life, suffice it to say, not in America, but in Argentina; he also knew that the neck of the American swan, the swan of the Columbian river and Patagonian lake, traced against the horizon, create the great question mark of freedom. (Will we be forced to speak English with so many millions of men?)

Rubén Darío's two prophecies come together for me while my eyes restlessly measure the grasslands in order to show the United States a power where it will be stopped. The Americas have nothing but the land of the pampa, populated solely by the white man.

There are two unparalled roads for the Atlantic and Pacific nations: to populate the land by organizing masses of strangers or to become organized and save themselves from the North.

February 1926

A WORD THAT WE HAVE STAINED:
TROPICALISM

Here we have one of those expressions in popular circulation which has been adapted and become an axiom. No one has wanted to examine it, not even in passing, in order to discuss its folly.

For the lazy, this expression has the advantage of brevity: they invoke tropicalism and avoid resounding censure. For the devotees of Taine, it is an irrevocable matter: exhuberant and splendid in nature: verbiage.

People from the cold lands utter this word, relishing it with childish glee . . . When I hear them, I think: Where are those tropical souls who write prose and verse congested with words? The first land that comes to mind is Mexico. Othón, whose verse is spare, almost hard; González-Martínez, the Athenian, Caso; Alfonso Reyes, Jenaro Estrada, López-Velarde, Tablada and all the new arrivals exhibit poetry and prose, measured and reduced like great heads on small medallions. I continue in the direction of Central America: there are Arévalo-Martínez, Turcios, Brenes Mesén, Heliodoro Valle, Molina and countless others. And I procede to Colombia and find Guillermo Valencia.

What is it then, this thing called tropicalism? It is not a verbal characteristic of hot climates but an expression of artistic cruelty directed against literatures in formation. Every prose or verse essayist is tropical, as is every writer from a culture which has not congealed and as is, finally, every man who expresses mental disorder, who seeks not to define or order, but who writes precipitately, without a code of honor. One must not forget that if it were a matter of tropical climates, Italy almost touches the tropics, and it produced Dante and Carducci, and it has Pascoli. The Castillian provinces, the plain, grey Castillian lands, and northern Spain, have given us thousands of insufferable poets of odes and hundreds of orators given to atrocious verbal excess.

Or is it possible that tropicalism is not a geographical zone, but rather a zone of the spirit, the zone of highest passion, the immense homeland of zealots? But this tropicalism is sometimes expressed with an imponderable sobriety. Pascal is sober and passionate; Saint Teresa comes across the same way in her verses.

No, tropicalism is literary babble turned bombastic by its sheer force and sometimes by vanity. It seeks energetic, or pictoral, or emotional expression, sentence by sentence, until it returns to the hydropic period.

And this tropicalism that links us as exclusively South American is Spanish and very Spanish, and it does not relate only to Spain's African feet.

And if tropicalism is the condition of the inflamed soul, then let it be blessed! Cool art is an intrusion with a profane end. What will they do with the flesh of poetry, these old ones with their icy hands of rhetoric? What trembling will their dead pulses communicate? Literature and music are the domains of the passionate, a tropical territory where the old smother.

As a tropical symbol, the ones who disdain it offer a sunflower-colored parrot. But why not the concise hummingbird? The tropics are not excessive, but intense. (Weigh the difference.) It is the precious stone into which fit all the colors spilled by the wide horizon. And the poet's tropical world is the same: rich in brevity, dense as a drop of resin.

This word tropicalism has been stained, like the word

"democracy," and like other words.

1922

AN INVITATION TO THE WORK
OF RAINER MARIA RILKE

The loving eye of the supernatural located within Rainer Maria Rilke's earthly self has closed. Death has paved the way for his translation into French, and month by month publishing houses are bringing out more of his books. But it would have been worthwhile to have given him the joy of this expansion into the language he loved more than his own: French. He was able to read only one selection in French: *Les Cahiers de Malte Laurids Brigge.*

Little fazed this ultra-aristocrat. He was a lover of all the lands he passed through and disdained the coteries which make fame an object of caustic stickiness in any land. But he would not have regarded his moderate glory in France in 1927 with indifference.

From time to time, in the fetid world of literature, some cases of genuine literary friendship still appear under the sign of lofty fellowship, for example, the friendships of Carlyle-Emerson or Goethe-Eckerman. Their discovering each other was like the pleasure of a plant lagging behind, holding onto its season: but that too vanishes.

In France, Rilke made two good friends, Edmond Jaloux and Paul Valéry. Jaloux passes as a disdainer of French literature by the power of his position as the best critic of foreign literature. He began to suffer attacks from "imperialists of the French language," and has spent ten years pointing out, through insistent citation, that Rilke is the premier German writer of his generation; he has just published a pamphlet about him. Valéry wrote to Rilke and expressed admiration of his translations into German.

French and German literary circles still reek with smothering vapors, and new values from the other side of the Rhine must travel uphill, proceeding toward France, and I do not mean the French people, in order to reach Berlin.

I do not believe in the Latin monopoly of masterworks, in accordance with Daudet's canon. The Holy Spirit has had the good taste not to take up residence in any of the intellectual capitals of xenophobic Europe and has moved with a disconcerting leap from Russia to India, to England, to France, and the United States.

Rilke was born into a noble family in Prague, around 1875. His portraits and a good bust of him show us an ascetic-looking man, a thin arrow of life, with an ample forehead, hard eyebrows softenend by the eyelids, somewhat dry cheeks, a virile, slightly thick mouth, and a Mongolian mustache, despite its blood tone. His eyes were clear and very gentle.

Also, like La Rochefoucauld, he wanted to leave us with a less pleasant medallion image, certainly differing in style from the French.

The persistence of old nobility could be found in the arc of his eyes. In his face, there still existed the fear and blue tint of infancy, and here and there, humility, but not the humility of a lackey but rather that of a servant and a woman. His mouth, the great and precise shape of his mouth, was not persuasive, but it expressed rectitude. The forehead lacked voluntary malice. His face tilted silently into the shadows.

"Like a woman," said Rilke, without fearing that the comparison would demean him. He has been called the poet of the child and the woman. He understood us better than the sensualists. It has been said that he who gets too close to an object ceases to see it. The memory of his own childhood helped him to love children. Does not the hardening that ruins us come when we forget this? Rilke remembered the child with marvelous tenderness, and this freed him from the monstrous condition of being entirely adult, absolute man or woman, without the golden fringe of telltale childlike qualities, without the elvish sands of a five-year old explorer swirling in the chambers of an old heart.

The few writers he approached, and those he allowed to get close to him, recall a man of extraordinary distinction, with kingly manners (if those of kings could measure up to his). Spirit truly poured into his body and face. His friendship was superior, difficult, as though in it he spent the same precious material he employed in a chapter or a strophe.

"The significance of an hour spent with Rilke, like one spent with Proust, does not resemble any hour spent with another man, not even with one of equal talent," said Jaloux.

For him poetry was not the hour of urgency in which the verse (or tense prose like verse) leaps forth from the man like the spark from a wheel; it was the day, the season, and the year.

He lived inside the electric cloud of his poetry, and getting close to him meant effectively leaving behind the atmosphere and coming to know the evident movement of the elements. Without didactics, he purified friendships by simple contact.

Such fellowship could not become democratic. Rodin, a man who enjoyed many gifts, also had it; Jaloux knew how to be worthy of it because his mind was swept free of envy. He will always allude to this fortune like someone who whirls a diamond in order to coax from it a free-spirited light show.

Rilke lived in Paris for more than ten years and took advantage of the great city as a place in the world where it is possible to find on the streets faces of those people who only inspire dreams, and thus he loved it, as did Baudelaire, living as the creator of the larvae he would have had to toil to produce in another setting. Nothing is known of his passage through Spain. He was a reserved man; the sun did not melt any part of him.

As a memeber of the ruling class, Rilke could have opted

for an admiralship, captainship, magistracy or cardinalship. He was placed, after all, in a school for cadets, about which he uttered words befitting the imbecility of many schools.

"This 'sabotage' called education, deprives a child of his own riches and replaces them with the mundane!"

He left behind his comrades in uniform and went on to studies in Germany which better suited him. At the age of eighteen, he published a rather weak book of premature verse; quite honestly, it sparked very little interest after it appeared. Immediately, a passion for travel began, and it would fill his life. Where didn't Rilke travel! He ventured to Italy, Spain, Egypt, Morroco, Scandinavia, Russia, Paris. Traveling, which generally has barbaric consequences, did not interrupt or disorder his inner life, which in any place is the only reality.

Nailed inside the house of his elders and relinquished to the beast of imagination, a man with a similarly tortured soul would have fallen prey to the morbid bitterness of Andreiff, from whom Rilke did acquire something of a passion for the mysteries of internalized pain. But he was freed from the demons of a sealed room by his journeys, which cut the violent and rough fabric of the world, setting images in motion.

Italy gave him the friendship of Eleonore Duse, but Italy was not his soul's climate. He believed that a princely ancestor had passed on to him a Nordic soul, and, according to Rilke, everything originated in the North. The hero of his masterpiece, Malte Brigge, would be Danish; he would call the teacher "Jacobsen." The folkloric genius of Selma Lagerloff would prove to be one of his most durable admirations, and to Helen Key he would dedicate his *Stories of a Good God*. One study of Rilke notes, ". . . in regard to his inner life, a tendency toward a Nordic temperment ruled over all pursuits."

Vasconcelos said that Latinity was lost and could no longer offer him anything. However, Rilke once wrote that among all poets, he would want to be Francis Jammes. Praise for his opposite, his absolute opposite! Jammes was almost botanical, a variety of masculine lemon tree, laden with fruits. He did not exert any possible influence on Rilke's spirit.

Critics have spoken and continue to speak about his work. Jaloux assures us that his influence on France has hardly begun, and it will last a long time. I only wanted to say something about his life and send *El Mercurio* pages of his *Stories of a Good God*, which still has not been translated into Spanish. It is his invitation to a complete reading, a search for friends among us.

A MESSAGE ABOUT PABLO NERUDA

Pablo Neruda, whom in Chile's Army Consulate we address as Ricardo Reyes, was born in the land of Parral, at the center of Chile's Llano Central, in 1904. We will always remember his coming as the birth of truth. The city of Temuco calls him its own and alleges the right of having given him the childhood that "imprinted the character" of his poetic soul. He studied literature at our Teacher's Institute in Santiago but was not moved to undertake the teaching vocation so common among Chileans. A minister who hardly suspected the optimal work that he was doing sent Neruda, at the age of twenty-three, on a consular mission to the Orient, placing great confidence in the brave youth. He lived in the Dutch Indies, Ceylon, and on islands in the Indian Ocean, a very special tropical zone. This occupied five years of Neruda's youth, engaging his sensibilities as if he had lived there for twenty years. But perhaps the strongest influences upon his temperment were these oceanic and sun-drenched lands, and English literature, which he understands and translates with inspired capacity.

Before leaving Chile, his book, *Crepusculario,* positioned him as the leader of his generation. Coming from the provinces and arriving in the capital, he discovered an alert group ready to liberate poetry through poetic reforms. The group, headed by Vicente Huidobro, the inventor of Creationism, expected sweeping results.

The work Neruda accomplished during the following years has just been gathered together with painstaking care by the Spanish publishing house Cruz y Raya into two very worthwhile volumes called *Residencia en la Tierra*. This work from the captain of our young people offers from its cover the grace and awe of its incisive title. *Residencia en la Tierra* will present all its students with a chain of poems to follow, link by link, the development of this formidable poet. True to himself and generous in regard to strangers, he offers his poems in scrupulous order—the amorphous and the elemental. They are products of a second style, until arriving at the ripe themes of wood, wine and celery. With slow and deliberate steps, one arrives at these three pieces, so masterfully anchored: a trio of substances. A reward is received: these poems are not only worthwhile as the work of an individual but can also fill the poetic needs of young people.

A spirit of the most inspired originality is making his way in search of what we call "expression," the achievement of a personal poetic language. He rejects those near him, that is to say, the nationals: the Pablo Neruda of this work shows no relationship with the Chilean lyric. He also rejects the greater part of foreign commerce; some contact with Blake, Whitman and Milosz, appear to be coincidence of temperment. Neruda's original diction, the adoption of a violent and raw vocabulary in the first place, corresponds with his nature, which in order to experience richness, must overflow to the point of nakedness. In the second place, it corresponds with a certain profession of faith which excludes preciousness. Neruda tends to assert that his generation has been freed, thanks to him, from neo-Gongorism. I do not know whether a defense of this infection would be good or bad; in any case, we will celebrate its appearance for having in some way sparked the magnificent vigor of our Neruda.

We imagine that Neruda's poetic style must scandalize those who write poetry of criticism according to a "beauty parlor style."

Neruda's stubborn expression is the mark of genuine Chilean idiosyncracy. Our people feel distant from highbrow poetry, and without a doubt, he feels the same artistic repulsion in regard to abstruse or flowery language. It is important to recall the sticky-sweet linguistic warehouse of "nightingales," "gauziness" and "roses" that left us mired in second rate *modernismo* in order to understand this gust of salty sea air with which Pablo Neruda cleanses his own sky and makes known his desire for clarification, in general.

Another side of Neruda's originality has to do with his themes. He has said farewell to our cloying poetic circumstances: twilight, seasons, idylls of the balcony and garden. This also, was jammed with stubborn customs and with inertia. The nature of a creator burns when he finds his subject matter in firewood and eggshells, and his subject matter must seem distasteful to those who trot along familiar paths. He gives us modern cities with grimacing, tortured souls, daily life in all its grotesqueness and misery, or the tenderness of something halting or ordinary. They are elegies in which death, treated in a new way, becomes an event we could not truly feel before. This is material treated with uncensored emotion, and it yields astonishing results: the end is presented to us through the putrefaction of all living and non-living things. Death is an insistent reference and almost an obsession in Neruda's work; he uncovers it for us and explores the most unlikely forms of ruin, agony and corruption.

Very little Spanish flavor can be extracted from Neruda's work, but it does have one very Castillean vein: a morbid obsession with death. The reader who is jarred by this might call Neruda an anti-mystic. We should be careful with the word mystic which we abuse so freely, frequently leaving us with a mere first impression. Neruda may be a mystic of the material world. Although we are discussing the ultimate poet of the body (he is Chilean, after all) following him, step by step, we discover in him this novelty which would hearten Saint John of the Cross: the material into which he plunges voluntarily quickly sickens him, and it is a repugnance that reaches the point of nausea. Neruda does praise material, he hammers it to pieces; he pommels it, and slits it open like a beast to better loathe it . . . And here an eternal bud of Castille is stripped naked.

His adventure with the material world seems to me a pure miracle. The Hindu monk, in agreement with M. Bergson, believes that to attain knowledge, we must truly get inside an object and see. In his song to wood, Neruda, a man of ineffable poetic operations, achieved this curious exile in a secret region apart from human experience.

The climate where the poet lives most of the time would have to be labelled dank and malarial. The poet, an eternally aborted angel, seeks a state of fevers to recreate his original element. He must also harbor some angelic spirits of the deep, one might call them, angels of caves or the sea bottom, because the plains that Neruda frequents seem more subterranean than atmospherical, despite the poet's oceanic passion.

He lives where he will and hurls messages to us; Pablo's acts of contemplation and respect flow from his personality. Neruda is America's new man. With his sensibilities, a new chapter of American emotions is being opened. His high rank is the result of a well-rounded, unique vision.

Various images leap up to me from Neruda's poetry as I finish reading and allow it all to settle in me. While I rest, it takes on an almost organic existence. This is one of those images: a tree, vexed by vines and mosses—it is simultaneously quiet, and quivering with vitality, within its boundary of appointed life. Some of his poems fill me with thunder, shaking and spasms of Nirvana, strangely sustaining a boiling point.

The opposing faculties and contrasted paths of the American soul are always explained by the *mestizo* factor; here as in any other case, it all comes down to a matter of bloodlines. Neruda gives credit to the white man, and also, equal time to the common *mestizo*, who, because of his European cultural vestiges, fabulously forgets his role as a double messenger. Neruda's Spanish friends smile affectionately at his ingenuous conviction. Although his body does not sufficiently reveal *mestizo* blood, his eyes and face, the langour of his gentures, and especially his speech, his poetry, so full of oriental vestiges, reveal the conflict in bloodlines—a blessing, this time. Blood mixing encompasses various aspects of pure tragedy; perhaps only in the arts does it present an advantage and provide the security of enrichment. In the richness that forms Neruda's emotional and linguistic alluvium, the confluence of a slightly brutal sarcasm, coupled with an almost religious seriousness, and in many more things, we witness the evident consequences of his tapestry of Spanish and Indian bloodliness. Any poet could be mesmerized by the spell of the Orient, but the Orient only helps partially, and then it perplexes; it does not offer friendship to the Westerner. Neruda's Indian clay came to a boil when he first touched Asia; *Residencia en la Tierra* tacitly recounts this deep encounter. It also exposes a secret: when a *mestizo* opens a dam, a torrent of originality is set free. Our imitation of America is painful; the journey back to being ourselves is a joyous undertaking.

But now let us consider the good word "Americanism." Neruda frequently recalls Whitman, in more ways than simply his use of verse made up of disproportionate vertebrae and the freedom of an American man who lived without fetters or obstructions. Americanism, in this work, is the resolution of vigor set free with luck, audacity, and a bitter fertility.

The latest poetry of the Americas (it cannot be classified as modernista or Ultraist) owes to Neruda something as important as justification for partial efforts. Neruda is coming after various waves of the poetic essay, which like a great tide thrust upon the coast the sea's entire visceral bounty. Some have lightly embraced it or hauled in parts of it.

My country owes Neruda extraordinary support: Chile has been a nation of fermentation and vigor, but its literature, for many years, was governed by a type of boar-toothed senate. It was classical in regard to its Beauty, and then pseudoclassical, but it hardly ever revealed a hint of the igneous heart of our race. Chile appears in anthologies as dry, obtuse and heavy. In *Residencia*, Neruda has allowed some tremendous Chilean yeast to rise and explode, assuring a poetic future, both wide in scope and ferocious.

April, 1936

HOW I WRITE

We women do not write only like Buffon, who for the critical moment would adorn herself with a lace-sleeved jacket and sit so very solemnly at her mahogany desk.

I write on my knees; the desk-table has never been of any use to me—not in Chile, Paris or Lisbon.

I write during the morning or night. The afternoon has never given me any inspiration; I do not understand the reason for its sterility or its lack of desire for me.

I believe that I have never written a verse in a closed room or in a room facing a drab wall of a house. I always seize a piece of sky: that which Chile gave to me with all blueness, Europe gives to me scribbled with clouds. My mood improves if I positively direct my old eyes and gaze at a mass of trees.

When I was a stable child of my race and country, I wrote about what I saw or what I possessed with immediacy: the warm flesh of the subject matter. Since I am a vagabond soul, in voluntary exile, it seems I only write from a central place, surrounded by a mist of ghosts. American lands, and my people, alive or dead, return to me in a melancholic and faithful procession; more than surrounding me, it encases me and oppresses me; rarely does it allow me to see the landscape and foreign people. Generally, I'm not in a hurry when I write; at other times, I write with the vertical speed of stones rolling down the cordillera. In any case, it irritates me when I have to stop; I always have four or six sharp pencils by my side because I am quite lazy. I've grown used to the luxurious habit of all being given to me complete, except the verses . . .

During the time when I battled with language, demanding its intensity, I tended to hear from myself a sufficiently angry gnashing of teeth, the fury of sandpaper over the blunt blade of words.

Now, I don't battle with words, but rather with something else . . . I've grown disgusted with and detached from my poems where I do not recognize spoken language, that which Don Miguel the Basque called "conversational language."

I revise more than people can believe, reading some verses which even in their corrected form seem rough to me. I left behind a labyrinth of hills, and something of this knot which cannot be unravelled remains in what I create, whether verse or prose.

Writing tends to cheer me; it always soothes my spirit and blesses me with the gift of an innocent, tender, childlike day. It is the sensation of having spent a few hours in my homeland, with my customs, free whims, my total freedom.

I like to write in a neat room, although I am a very disorganized person. The order seems to give me space; my eyes and soul have this appetite for space. Sometimes I've written following the rhythm I gathered from a channel of water flowing down the street beside me—or I've followed nature's sounds. All melt within me and form a kind of cradle song.

On the other hand, I still have anecdotal poetry, which young poets disdain very much.

Poetry comforts my senses and that which is referred to as "the soul"—but another's poetry more than my own. Both make my blood flow better. They defend the childlike quality of my character, rejuvenate me, and make me feel a sort of asepsia in regard to the world. Poetry simply exists within me, and on my lap; it is the thirst of a submerged childhood. Although the result is bitter and hard, the poetry I make cleanses me of the world's dust and even the inscrutable, essential vileness similar to what we call original sin. I carry it with me; I carry it with affliction. Perhaps original sin is nothing more than our fall into the rational and anti-rhythmic expression which has lowered the human race. It hurts us women more because of the joy we lost, the grace of a musical and intuitive language that was going to be the language of the human race.

This is all I know how to articulate about my experience. Do not force me to discover more . . .

ABOUT THE TRANSLATOR

Maria Giachetti (Jacketti) was born in 1960 in Hazelton, Pennsylvania. In addition to being a translator, she is also a fiction writer, poet, and college instructor. She has translated Pablo Neruda's *Las piedras del cielo, Heaven Stones* (Cross Cultural Communications); a selection of Neruda's botanical odes, *Neruda's Garden* (Latin American Literary Review Press); *Cantos Ceremoniales, Ceremonial Songs* (Latin American Literary Review Press) and *Maremoto, Seaquake* with Dennis Maloney (White Pine Press). Her first collection of poetry, *Black Diamond Madonna,* was published by Cross Cultural Communications.

Ms. Giachetti is a recipient of a poetry fellowship from the Pennsylvania Council on the Arts. She holds a bachelor's degree with majors in French, Spanish, and mass communications from King's College in Wilkes-Barre, Pennsylvania, and a master's degree in creative writing from New York University.

ABOUT THE EDITOR

Marjorie Agosin is a native of Chile who now lives in Wellesley, Massachusetts, where she teaches Latin American literature at Wellesley College. Agosin has long been an advocate of human rights and much of her work focuses on the human rights abuses that have taken place in her native country and throughout Latin America. Her poetry powerfully portrays the guilt of those who chose to look away, the suffering of the oppressed and their families, and the brutality of their tormentors. Agosin's work, both as poet and as editor, has received wide critical acclaim. She has traveled throughout the United States and Latin America delivering lectures and reading her work. She has also made many television appearances.

Her published works include *Scraps of Life*, essays on the Chilean *arpilleras; Latin American Women in Literature; Zones of Pain; Women of Smoke; Bonfires;* and *Circles of Madness*, a bilingual book of poetry documenting the Mothers of the Plaza de Mayo featuring the photographs of Alicia D'Amico and Alicia Sanguinetti. As the White Pine Press Latin American editor, Marjorie Agosin has edited the following volumes: *Landscapes of a New Land: Short Fiction by Latin American Women;* and *Secret Weavers: Stories of the Fantastic by Women of Argentina and Chile. Scraps of Life* was made into a half-hour documentary and shown on PBS. She was the recipient of the Janette Rankin Foundation's award for work in the areas of women and nonviolence.

THE SECRET WEAVERS SERIES
Series Editor: Marjorie Agosín

Dedicated to bringing the rich and varied writing by Latin American women to the English-speaking audience.

Volume 11
A NECKLACE OF WORDS
Short Fiction by Mexican Women
152 PAGES $14.00

Volume 10
THE LOST CHRONICLES OF TERRA FIRMA
A Novel by Rosario Aguilar
192 pages $13.00

Volume 9
WHAT IS SECRET
Stories by Chilean Women
304 pages $17.00

Volume 8
HAPPY DAYS, UNCLE SERGIO
A Novel by Magali García Ramis
Translated by Carmen C. Esteves
160 pages $12.00

Volume 7
THESE ARE NOT SWEET GIRLS
Poetry by Latin American Women
368 pages $17.00

Volume 6
PLEASURE IN THE WORD
Erotic Fiction by Latin American Women
Edited by Margarite Fernández Olmos & Lizabeth Paravisini-Gebert
240 pages $19.95 cloth

Volume 5
A GABRIELA MISTRAL READER
Translated by Maria Giacchetti
232 pages $15.00

Volume 3
LANDSCAPES OF A NEW LAND
Short Fiction by Latin American Women
194 pages $12.00

THE STONES OF CHILE
Poems by Pablo Neruda
Translated by Dennis Maloney
98 pages $10.00   Bilingual

SARGASSO
Poems by Marjorie Agosín
Translated by Cola Franzen
92 pages $12.00   Bilingual

LIGHT AND SHADOWS
Poems by Juan Ramon Jimenez
Translated by Robert Bly, Dennis Maloney, Clark Zlotchew
70 pages $9.00

VERTICAL POETRY
Poems by Roberto Juarroz
Translated by Mary Crow
118 pages $11.00   Bilingual

SELECTED POEMS OF MIGUAL HERNANDEZ
Translated by Robert Bly, Timothy Baland, Hardi St Martin and James Wright
138 pages $11.00   Bilingual